THE HAMSTER THAT LOVED PUCCINI

The Hamster that Loved Puccini

THE SEVEN MODERN SINS OF CHRISTMAS ROUND ROBIN LETTERS

Simon Hoggart

Atlantic Books
London

Published in hardback in Great Britain in 2005 by Atlantic Books.
Atlantic Books is an imprint of Grove Atlantic Ltd.

ISBN 1 84354 474 1

A CIP catalogue record for this book is available from the British Library.

Typeset by Avon DataSet Ltd, Bidford on Avon, Warwickshire

Printed in Great Britain by CPD, Ebbw Vale, Wales
Text design by Lindsay Nash

Atlantic Books
An imprint of Grove Atlantic Ltd
Ormond House
26–27 Boswell Street
London
WC1N 3JZ

Contents

Introduction

IT IS SAD for us aficionados of the Christmas circular letter, but I fear that it is true – the writers are getting terrifically self-conscious. They have developed a little censor in their brains, rather like the seven-second tape loop some phone-in radio stations use to stop people swearing on air. They have begun to think that they ought not to be too boastful, should devote less time to their exotic foreign holidays, or the many talents of their children, or the building works that have converted their home into a new Xanadu. They have come to feel that they ought to mix in some bad news with the good. They have adopted, in some cases, a tone of jovial self-deprecation. 'We shouldn't really be telling you this, but I'm sure Amanda won't mind us letting you know that she got more starred As than anyone else in her class...' Or, 'at the risk of sounding complacent about our new home – yippee!'; 'The holiday of a lifetime turned into something of a nightmare...'; 'the builders having gone, we woke up one morning to find that the conservatory floor had opened up leaving a gaping hole, big enough for the entire family to stand up in...' I have made those up, but it does give you the flavour.

Or take the amused tone of the letter which gives this book its title. The writers say that they are opera fans, and listen to opera at home. Their children's hamster sits still or nibbles quietly on its food while Verdi, Wagner or Mozart CDs are playing; when they play songs by Puccini, by contrast, the little chap leaps on to his wheel and begins joyful spinning.

Clearly we are not meant to take this story all that seriously, even if the writers have observed the phenomenon from time to time. The message they are sending is: 'Look, we're light-hearted folk; we may be opera lovers, but we have a sense of humour!'

Many writers these days make jovial remarks about how boring the newsletters can be. 'Sorry to inflict this on you, but it's the only way we can keep in touch. Please feel free to throw away unread!' is a typical comment. They are more judicious now in telling us about their children's numerous successes, academic, musical and sporting.

Some have become rather defensive. This is from a British family living in the Middle East:

> I WAS *delighted to have caused so much dialogue amongst those who abhor round robins, and found it hilarious that some people were totally disgusted by this lazy woman who could not find the time to put pen to paper on an individual basis. Well, guys, I am rather tied up with being a wife to my husband, a mother to my children and making money for my boss. So please bear with me,*

and hopefully when I'm retired and a grandmother, I'll be able to oblige – that's if the arthritis hasn't set in by then!!

Another letter complains bitterly about the contumely heaped upon circular newsletters, then spoils the whole effect by duplicating the customs stamps they had gathered through the year – from Los Angeles, New Zealand, Australia, Polynesia, the Cook Islands and Singapore – just in case we needed reminding about their amazing travels.

Yet another newsletter enquired in passing whether all *Guardian* readers – they have sent in around half the letters used in this book – are people-haters. (Answer: no, just antipathetic to those who feel obliged to forward every single detail of their lives on the assumption that the recipients care, or even have time to look.) They go on to ask whether they are made up. (Answer: no, and even if I had been tempted, it would be impossible to invent anything approaching the gusto, the fascination and the surreal quality of the genuine article.) They also ask, a little plaintively, why, if the recipients of round robin letters dislike them so much, 'and with such venomous energy, could they not have directed their hate mail to the Bush camp, where at least it would have been well deserved?' (Answer: we are all angered by many things, including perhaps the war in Iraq, an unwanted branch of Tescos opening, and round robin letters from people we haven't seen for more than thirty years. The difference is that there is little any of us can do about the first two.)

The last letter includes, a little sadly I feel, a slip at the bottom marked 'don't continue to send me Xmas letters', with space for a signature, but as the reader who passed it on to me points out, 'to say you no longer wish to receive their letters could be very hurtful'. Which is true, though I suspect she may be missing the point; the writers offered the opportunity knowing that few if any of their recipients would take it up, and so have awarded themselves the right to continue sending the letters.

I find I do not hate the round robins quite as much as do the people who send them on to me. In fact I don't hate them at all. I like nearly all of them, and some I think are wonderful. This may be because I don't know the writers. If, for example, you did meet the husband briefly at a conference in Bristol twenty years ago, but have never had any contact with him since, it must be peculiarly infuriating to hear news of his family, none of whom you have ever met. Getting the letter at second hand removes the sense of resentment, the annoying feeling some recipients have that their homes have been invaded by people who wish to reveal to them how inferior their lives are.

Some people compound the offence by appending great lists of names (there are several in this book) without any indication of who the people are or what role they have in the writers' lives. It's usually possible to work out who the children are, if only because they merit so much space, but to be told apropos of nothing that Les and Jakki have just taken delivery of a new Jaguar (in racing green, no less!) without having the faintest idea who Les and Jakki might be, is enough to drive anyone into a gasping, air-clawing rage. (I have changed all of the names in these letters, while trying to stick to the same age and class. So Ediths don't become Sharons, though a Bruno might well become a Tarquin. I have also changed place names where they might identify the writers, though of course a trip to Paris remains a trip to Paris.)

Personally I enjoy the letters on several levels. I am reminded of those early autumn evenings, when people turn the lights on in their front rooms but fail to draw the curtains. Without actually stopping in the street to stare, you can glimpse tableaux from people's lives: a couple sitting cosily on the sofa, a drinks party, a family quarrel. In that half second you can get a brief but fascinating insight into the lives of others and catch sight of their private faces. How much more can you learn from a Christmas newsletter – not, perhaps, from the account of their annual activities, but the characters and attitudes that are revealed. In spite of the new self-consciousness that has crept in, people do tend to be fairly unguarded when they sit down at their computer keyboard to write.

I sometimes think of the letters as if they were short novels with a large and colourful cast of characters. No one reading *The Darling Buds of May* would say: 'I hate these Larkins, with their endless jollity, their wonderful holidays, their oh-so-marvellous children and that ghastly father who clearly thinks he is some kind of lovable rogue when he is really just a drunken old bore…'

Nor would you read *Madame Bovary* with the same baleful eye as round robin recipients. 'I knew this doctor when I worked for a year in northern France. He was pretty incompetent as I recall, and the wife certainly looked like trouble to me. I am sorry their lives have worked out so badly, but heavens, must I be told every single detail? As for the boy with the club foot – too much information!'

Sometimes the letters read like one of those experimental novels in which the pages are kept loose and shuffled, so the story can be read in an entirely haphazard fashion. The result is that important events appear apparently at random and in unpredictable order: the refurbished rockery and the weekend in Prague may be followed by the death of a beloved parent; news of the couple divorcing is somehow squeezed between the A-levels and the loft extension.

Some of this sense of the letters being an extended work of fiction came in a covering letter from North London, whose author I won't name since it reveals the fact that he had shopped one of his friends:

THESE CHRISTMAS *round robins are usually one of a sequence, sometimes stretching back twenty years and more. The characters in*

them, the complacent holiday-going couple, the perfect children,
the accident-prone relative — like the dramatis personae of a long-
running soap, become archetypal, behaving more and more as you
expect them to do as the years pass. We have a friend who lives in a
small village who each year sends us what is, in effect, a short story
concerning the doings of the village inhabitants, featuring the
grasping-but-thick innkeeper, the bumbling parson, the village
joker, et al. Funnier than the EastEnders *Christmas special . . .*

David Skidmore of St Albans forwarded an article by an American writer, Suzanne Perez Tobias, who offers tips on writing what she calls holiday letters, all of them sound. Her advice can be summed up as 'keep it snappy, keep it short, keep it interesting'. Consider your audience, since not everyone wants to know every detail of your life. Explain who people are, so instead of saying baldly 'Jane had a baby', write 'my sister Jane had a baby'. Don't be cute: wise advice for the many people who imagine their letter will be the more beguiling as if written by the family pet. Don't brag about everything. 'If you ran a marathon or wrote a book, by all means say so. Just keep it real… on the other hand, don't be too real. Nobody wants to hear every gruesome detail of your periodontal surgery or the things you've learned about projectile vomiting…'

A surprising number of letters stick to these principles. Of the several hundred that are sent to me every year, around 40 per cent don't contain any usable nuggets, though often it is the cumulative effect that grates, so that by the end, even if there is no single rage-inducing moment, the reader casts the thing aside with an exasperated sigh. Why on earth do they imagine that we care?

On the other hand, thank heavens, many people do drop their guard often enough to allow the reader a shout of glee, which is why sorting through hundreds of letters every year is something I enjoy very much. My favourites here include the telepathic rabbit, the travails of a socialist landlord, the man obsessed with his study of Tasmanian cycling strategy, the holidaymakers who describe every single detail of their lives, including the positioning of the brake in their hire car – and, of course, the hamster that loved Puccini.

While reading this year's crop, I realized that there are roughly six elements that make round robin letters so infuriating: descriptions of wonderful children; accounts of equally fabulous holidays (and other elements in their lives that make the writers so pleased with themselves); those offering far more detail than anyone could possibly want to read; those inflicting all the miseries that the writers have suffered through the year, often also recounted in mind-numbing detail; proselytizing religion in which the writers' lives act as texts for the promulagation of their religious beliefs; and – in some ways the worst of the lot – whimsy, the desperate attempt to make a newsletter more exciting by putting the words into the mouths of a family pet – even, in some cases, a dead one.

Since this makes only six deadly sins, I have added hatred – the wicked, but often entirely understandable emotion that grips the readers when they first receive these letters and, with shaking hand, stuff them into an envelope and send them on to me. To all these recipients, thank you. The book would not have been possible without your help.

The extracts from the letters are all as they were written, except for some very minor grammatical changes to make them easier to follow.

The Peccadillo of Proud Parenthood

OF ALL THE SINS committed by the senders of Christmas newsletters, an excessive admiration for their offspring is probably the worst – certainly the one most likely to drive recipients into a demented rage. What is it with these children, with their perfect exam results, their thespian abilities, sporting talent, musical genius and part-time charity work? Don't they ever get drunk at a friend's house, watch too much television, smoke pot or even answer back? Do none of them wear hoodies, or swear, or eat junk food instead of tofu sandwiches? I suspect what makes these children so infuriating is the knowledge that most of them probably do some of those things; it's just that their parents have decided to ignore such topics for the purpose of the Christmas letter. And, since we can presume that most of the children see the letters, the writers see it as an easy way to earn parental brownie points – 'of course she knows how much we admire what she does; we put it in this year's letter, didn't we?'

None of this can be much consolation to those who receive the bulletins.

MY EARS ringing with praise of Jake from his teachers at our termly parent–teacher evening, I got home to find Emily opening a letter telling her that she had won a place at Oxford! To read medicine, no less! Gordon Brown, eat your heart out. It is a four-year course, so she has had to postpone her gap year in Latin America.

To which the only possible response is 'Oh no, must you do this to us?'

CHLOE *wins the prize for most activities. In music, she continues with the recorders, violin and piano and has now taken up the flute as well. She is in the Junior School orchestra and wind band. Recently she had an audition for the national preparation schools orchestra, was selected for the orchestra itself (violin) and so will spend a week in Norfolk next summer. She also won cups at school for the best string player, and as a member of the top ensemble. After-school activities include netball, gymnastics, tap, ballet, tennis and Girl Guides. In swimming she won a gold medal at the county age group championships as a member of the relay team and has represented her club and school in many galas. She also has had one of her works of art mounted in the entrance foyer of the school. As a postscript, school work seems to be progressing without noticeable effort.*

You have to feel sorry for her younger brother, Ifan, who is 'alto-gether more laid back... he very much enjoys relaxing at home, goes to bed late and gets up late...' Suspicions grow in the reader's mind. Is Ifan not an achiever like his big sister? Not an achiever? Are you mad?

> *Earlier this year Ifan played from memory the slow movement of the Rachmaninov piano concerto no. 2 at a school concert, and later won the Junior Mozart Cup at our city music festival. He will play bassoon for the under-21 wind band, and will go on a concert tour this summer in Paris and the Loire Valley. He very much enjoys tennis, swimming, hockey and also plays bridge for the school...*

Of course he does. In fact, it is something of a surprise that any of the other pupils get a look in.

This is from America, where if anything the sin of overweening parental pride is even more widespread.

> *OUR CHILDREN continue to be a source of infinite joy. Taylor is thriving in kindergarten, and we all just shake our heads in amazement at his development. He loves school, and his teacher, Mrs Shannon. He is already reading second and third-grade readers and whips through books at lightning speed. He loves to go to the library and get out stacks of books... he loves to read aloud to us and he does so with a great deal of expression and drama. Despite his reading ability he actually enjoys math more. He sits in his car seat (a bit small for his four foot, seventy pound frame) as we drive to Pittsburgh on our many excursions to the city and we play math word games ('when you're twenty years old, how old will Monica*

be?') He invariably gets them right. On one famous occasion as we emerged from the Fort Pitt Tunnel and Pittsburgh came into view, Taylor said, 'Ah, civilization!' . . . after some initial resistance he has taken to the violin like a fish to water. During a recital at school, he was actually tuning the piano, a feat which impressed his mother and teacher both. He will be starting group and theory sessions in the New Year at the music academy. In case you hadn't noticed, we're very proud of Taylor.

Again some poor younger child is reduced to playing second fiddle to the great violinist:

Monica has come on by leaps and bounds. We would like to report that she is potty trained and weaned from her 'binky' [excuse me?] *but we have met with some resistance . . . Monica has gravitated to her dolls and strollers and (ugh! Dare I say it?) Barbies. We are glad she outgrew her macabre habit of scattering her disrobed dollies all round the house then covering them with dishtowels, faces and all . . .*

Our in-house psychiatrist writes: 'for a pre-school child to surround herself with images of death implies a latent but powerful resentment, even hatred for another family member. It is not yet clear who . . .'

So many small geniuses, so little time.

TORI *has been doing incredibly well at school, winning the gym cup, physics cup, history cup and heaven knows what else. In her spare time she's been dancing, doing drama and learning to play the cello. Loads of her friends came along for her Friends-theme birthday party, with a room at the youth centre turned into 'Central Perk' for the afternoon... Maddie is a little star, with incredible writing, drawing and other skills. She made a lovely angel in the nativity play – all blonde hair and golden costumes. The big house news is that we finally felt it safe enough to buy carpets...*

JOEL *has become the city's Tae-Kwan Do Student of the Year.*

KEIRA *has soldiered on throughout all this* [her brother suffers from lacto-intolerance and her father had chest pains, but it turned out nothing was seriously wrong] *studying for five Highers – Physics, Chemistry, English, Maths and Modern Studies. She did extremely well in her Standard grades, getting straight grade ones. She did her bronze Duke of Edinburgh award this year, and plans to go on to do silver. She goes to the gym, does yoga, shops and watches a lot of TV. We are lucky in that her schoolwork is always done first. She is now taller than both Ted and me!*

Here's a welcome example of a younger child who, if anything, is even more outstanding than his older sibling – studying at a school which is a 'national centre of excellence' with a 'top 50 rating for achievement'.

WE ARE delighted to report that Fraser has thrived in this formal grammar school environment, particularly in relation to his personal development, self-confidence, time management (up to twenty-two pieces of homework a week!), mathematics, basketball, humanities and French. Outside academia, each Saturday morning he excels as a teaching assistant for two classes of children who find swimming a challenge. In addition, Wednesday evening's hour and half training sessions have yielded lifesaving awards. Despite bouts of eczema, Fraser has focused his sprinting skills in playing 'up front' for his local football team. Well done, keep up the brilliant work!

Why they need to exhort their son in a newsletter written for people outside the family is not made clear. Still, if you think that Fraser sounds pretty well perfect, meet his little brother Dan:

Congratulations to Dan, nine, for working hard, digging in his bag of grit and determination at his gift for running and ignoring his hay fever with a victory, despite falling, in the inter-schools athletics championship in the 800m. After an autumn of training, Dan represented his school in the under-tens cross-country championship — with 250 runners his second competitive season of races resulted in a fifteenth, seventh, and in the final race, a VICTORY! As a result of this achievement he has been invited to join the county athletics club. He continues to thrive in the swimming pool, earning his Silver and Gold personal survival and 3,000m awards. At school he remains a 'ray of sunshine' in his

gifted and talented class. At Cubs, Dan is a seconder, has an arm
full of proficiency badges and a perfected talent for getting very
muddy on the many weekend trips to camps, castles and Outward
Bound courses.

The temptation to write back, describing your own children's hopeless results and their practice of lying slumped in front of the TV every night and all weekend, is very great. Certainly few people put that kind of thing in their newsletters.

GCSE results come through, so it's all a bit tense with our first child
doing public exams. Laura sends me a text message which says
'eleven A-stars'. Assumed that with thirty years of grade inflation
this is equivalent to my grade 7 failure at Italian O-level. But when
Laura shows me her name in the local newspaper, there is only one
other kid in the county mentioned in the 'eleven A-stars'
category...

Grandparents are every bit as proud of their offspring's offspring:

ANTONIA, our oldest granddaughter, at seven, is old enough to be
taken to things, and she enjoyed her first opera, The Magic Flute, at
the ENO, and Midsummer Night's Dream at the open-air theatre in
Regents Park. We enjoyed her enjoyment! ... she has just acquired
her first LAMDA certificate — with distinction, of course — and we
all have to get up next Sunday to hear her sing the Magnificat solo

*in church! Brief conversation between Betty and Toni in respect of
all this:*

*BETTY: well, done, Toni, another certificate! I expect your Mummy
has a file for all these!*

ANTONIA: Oh yes, Granny, and it's bulging!

Christabel, the eighteen-month old, is another little saint...

JEB *has been typing for Britain this year, as it is now necessary that
he use a laptop in the classroom. We have all benefited from this,
and are all regularly to be found practising our touch typing skills!
For the second year running, he was awarded the school's prize for
outstanding effort, and this was presented to him by Cardinal
Cormac Murphy O'Connor* [Archbishop of Westminster] *at
school. He has gained his Grade 3 in saxophone, and will be taking
Grade 3 oboe in the spring, and has joined the school orchestra.
This year has seen a new interest — fencing, for which he seems to
have endless enthusiasm.*

Some parents devote many hundreds of words to the multitudi-
nous successes of their children. This one features large pictures
of each child, with a lengthy description of their talents:

AT SCHOOL, *Ferdie continues to do exceptionally well,
particularly in maths and English. He has also stuck with the cello,
and can now bash out a passable Beethoven's ninth, without music
to read... Sean is beginning to develop artistic talents and won a*

prize in the county arts festival this year. His picture, which was a
scene from a legend around the creation of our lake, was mounted
and hung in the new village hall for the duration of the festival...

Once again, it's the youngest who may be giving cause for anxiety. Few academic or artistic triumphs here, but it is a poor parent who cannot find a biscuit amid the bran:

Gemma has turned into a delightful chatterbox, though she does
boss the boys around!

These parents, who live in Queensland, Australia, are so fascinated by their own children that they want to pass on every single thing they do:

NAOMI *continues to grow taller and more beautiful by the day. She*
is rapidly turning into a young woman. She has just finished Grade
7 at her state school, where she has had a wonderful seven years,
with great teachers, an excellent principal, a group of close and
delightful friends, and she has finished her Grade 7 with an
exceptionally good report card which confirms her talent and
ability, and the quality of teaching and the school.

During the year she went to music camp, playing viola,
changing piano teachers, but still managed a credit for her piano
exam, sang beautifully in the school choir, and headed off for an
exciting school trip to Sydney and Canberra. Played the lead role
(Cinders) in Cinderella, a modern re-telling of the Cinderella story,

played her viola in the school orchestra, and received a Junior
Rotary Award for various activities, including community service.

At which point the average reader may feel he already knows
enough about Naomi's year. But her mum and dad have barely got
started.

The big news is that, after a reassessment of what would best suit
Naomi's talents and abilities, we have enrolled her at St Aloysius, a
Catholic girls' school (no, she's not a Catholic) which we believe is
going to be a great secondary school for her. St Aloysius is on a hill
at Tuckamarra . . . we have already been to the orientation day,
purchased the uniforms, books and bag, and the dates are on the
calendar.

This is the point at which one wonders whether it might be time
to put down the letter and perhaps take up a su doku puzzle
instead. Because there is more, much more, to come:

. . . Both her grandmothers continue to delight in her company.
The last of her two guinea pigs, and one replacement, died this
year, so now we have two new frisky young guinea pigs in the
hutch! Caspar the budgie continues to be happy, and noisy! The
fish, however, didn't make it through the year. Replacement coming
soon.

Keep us posted! These people live on a farm in Yorkshire:

THE STRINGS *of rosettes decorating the kitchen are fuller than ever this year… Jack is heading for the Arctic Circle in northern Sweden in January for a six-month project protecting arboreal forests. After that, the world is his ostrich… alas, we have lost one colony of bees this autumn, after an attack on their hive by sheep.*

What so infuriated the sheep is left unexplained.

BEATRICE *and Belinda continue to make their parents excessively proud. Friends will know that B1 has been in China, and returns from there at the end of January, having successfully opened, run, and sold 'the London café' in Guangdong. She is, also, down to the halfway point in the tedious selection process to work in the EU. This means she has already beaten 3,500 other candidates… B2 continues to save the world, with increasing intensity. This year it has been street children and HIV/AIDS victims in Ethiopia… she has been awarded the Malcolm Deaver Memorial Award at her college, and a Mansfield Award for Excellence and Achievement (runner-up Student of the Year award) for the University as a whole.*

PHILOMENA *(Philly), with her thick auburn hair cut into a very becoming short style (all part of the tomboy look), is growing up rapidly and delightfully and has a great zest for life. Her bedroom is plastered with pictures of wild animals. She has a hamster called Zebediah Jones, and her hobbies are 'animals, drawing animals and*

*birds, reading and dreaming about going to Africa and South
America, where lots of animals, rainforests and birds are'. She is a
voracious reader (had a passion for pigs, until she read Animal
Farm), and has done exams in drama, violin and piano
(distinction!) But we are not in the business of league tables, and
always vowed that ours would not be that kind of Christmas letter.*

Sorry, too late!

But people are growing increasingly conscious that – even if
nothing will stop them listing their children's talents and successes
– some form of apology is required. This is from the East Midlands:

*RUTHIE (ten) is in her final year at primary school and doing very
well. Listing her other activities makes us seem 'pushy' parents, but
honestly we're not! We just work on the principle that children are
at their best when occupied elsewhere. Ruthie goes dancing (ballet,
tap, modern, ballroom and disco), does swimming, gymnastics, has
violin and piano lessons, belongs to a string orchestra, to Girl
Guides and to the Girls' Brigade... she is preparing for
Confirmation next year, as an Anglican, a Roman Catholic, or
both. Artie (eight) is also doing very well in school... the football
team he played for last season won their league. Edward is the
striker and scored a hat trick today. Proud Daddy on the touchline.*

Sometimes children do have to settle for second best. Here's one
who did not get sufficient A-stars in his GCSEs, and is now shelf-

stacking for Tesco on Friday evenings and Sunday afternoons.

> HE HAD *one lady ask him if Tesco's sold panty-liners for thongs — I*
> *ask you! — and another who wanted salt without any additives, and*
> *when he found her one, she read the label and complained that it*
> *contained sodium chloride!*

Children can bring unwanted distress:

> PETER *performing as a young preacher's son called Willem in the*
> *rather gruesome opera* Batavia *for the arts festival. It was most*
> *disconcerting to watch your son drowned in the orchestra pit only*
> *to become the butcher's son (with a wig) and be murdered again in*
> *the Third Act. I cried the whole way through the opera.*

This letter is another from Australia, a land which seems to foster
a special interest in gore.

> HAMISH *is very interested in film-making, editing and that sort of*
> *stuff. He is good at it too. He did a week's work experience with one*
> *of the local television stations and really enjoyed it... He was most*
> *disappointed that the news clip of a fatal car accident he went to*
> *with one of the cameramen did not show the pool of blood that they*
> *had filmed.*

The whole family sounds pretty bloodthirsty — later:

> *Our old dog, Zippy, has not been too well, with colitis and arthritis,*

WE HAD *a great summer holiday in Canada and the US, and Clem had a lovely time, meeting lots of people and having lots of fun. Clem left for Canada with four teeth, and came home with a complete smile-full!!*

CAMERON, *eight, is a bit of a mimic and can recite lines from movies, with a speciality being death scenes in war movies and Joey in Friends episodes! He loves model-making and any card or unwanted boxes (which we have in abundant supply) quickly gets converted into castles, ammunition depots, dens, look-outs, spaceships. He also loves playing with Brigit, who idolizes him. Recently I asked Cameron what he wanted to do when he was older. He clasped his hand to his chest and after a few minutes of silence, I prompted him again, and he replied, 'I am still listening to my heart, Mummy.'*

This family cannot wait even for the birth of the new prodigy. They sent a remorseless succession of e-mails about the arrival of their first-born.

FOR SOME *of you this will be the first mail from Terry and myself regarding the not too distant birth of Baby Brown, the first Spooner grandchild! With just under six weeks to go, I thought I would get a move on with contact lists and e-mail groupings to make it easier for Terry to spread the word on the day. Watch this space, for more news as it breaks!*

Six weeks later the glad tidings arrive:

> *Patricia and I are amazed and delighted to announce the birth of*
> *Danielle Eve Brown… picture of proud parents and our adorable*
> *daughter attached.*

One month after that:

> *Just thought I'd take this opportunity to send a quick update and a*
> *couple of photos taken of Danielle over the Christmas period and*
> *yesterday, on her one-month birthday… luckily it looks as if she*
> *has taken on her dad's more chilled-out character. First photo*
> *obviously taken on Christmas Day — Santa's little helper!*

> *Can't believe another month has passed — second photo shows a*
> *smiling Danielle on her two-month birthday.*

This is followed, as ever, by an update on the baby's weight, her
sleep patterns, and her injections.

> *She continues to delight and amaze us, as she's far more interactive*
> *now. Those of you who know my obsession with taking photos won't*
> *be disappointed as the album is growing rapidly with all her little*
> *'firsts'.*

They are back a month later, to bring the hot news that Danielle
is now 12lb 3oz, and refusing to feed from a bottle. She has been
moved into her own room, and has been taken on a trip to meet

her grandparents in the north, though the journey was disrupted by a puncture.

Then comes next month's e-mail, marked by its recipient: 'Just when I thought it couldn't get any worse...' Danielle has decided to man the keyboard herself:

> *Now that I'm four months old, I've even got my own e-mail address, so I thought I would send this month's update straight from the horse's mouth, so to speak! I'm still growing at such a rate, but don't have an exact weight as mummy has been told I don't need to be weighed in clinic as often cos I'm doing so well... this month has seen the introduction of a door bouncer...*

Presumably one of those elasticated harnesses children play in, rather than a burly man with a cheap suit and an earpiece. The precocious baby continues:

> *I also got to spend more time with my second cousin Steffie, who is just six months older than me. It's nice to have another 'little person' around as well as the boring adults and I can't wait until Uncle Rob's baby arrives in August. We're going to have so much fun!*
>
> *I guess that just about sums up my antics this month. Enjoy the photos. More news soon.*

To which the recipient has appended a simple but heartfelt 'Aarrghhh!'

Getting your infant child to write the newsletter is a more

frequent practice. It is deeply annoying habit.

> MUM *stopped working in mid-March in preparation for the big day. She had two weeks off before I was born by elective caesarean on April 5th. I had a rather important birth notice: I got on the cover of a national magazine after I was born because apparently the way that I was conceived was pretty special...*

This is not explained. Test tube? Turkey baster? Virgin birth?

> *... I even got to go to Sydney with Mum and Dad later in the year to appear on a television programme on IVF...*

Ah.

> *I got to meet Professor Lord Robert Winston, and we had our photo in another magazine. I guess that you could say that I have been a bit of a media superstar already!*

As children grow older they can genuinely write – and boast – for themselves. In this family everyone chips in:

> CHRISTABEL: *At the end of last year I finished by mentioning my Grade three cello exams, which were to come in the next couple of days, so I am very pleased to say I passed with 109! For just over a year now I have been swimming for our local swimming club, it is such good fun, and I have made loads of new friends. I am now in the top squad along with Fergus, and I am continually breaking my*

personal best times, which is good. Coming up is the Christmas Disco and presentation evening, so I will be coming away with a few medals.

This letter is from a child in South Africa.

SCHOOL *has been going very well for me. I have started my coursework and have not found it as difficult as I expected… I have completed two pieces, in both of which I got A grades… we recently had a debate on whether migration does more harm than good. I was on the against team and was told that I gave a very good case with witty answers… I am playing the drums and may take the first grade early next year. My teacher is very pleased with my progress. He has mentioned that I have the ability to play other percussion instruments and have a bizarre skill that enables me to play with my left hand as if I was ambidextrous. The budgie is well and happy after I gave him a honey stick as an early Christmas present.*

Tragically not all children are as admirable, and now and again their parents feel obliged to vent their feelings.

WE ARE *finding this stage of the terrible two's rather wearing and tiring, although we are beginning to see chinks of light here and there, although potty training remains an issue four months on… yes, FOUR MONTHS!!! (Caroline took only two weeks!) We started the task during the summer holidays, but although he'll sit*

*on the potty and see results time after time after time, he just won't
ask to use it. We got so fed up with the fact that he went through all
his trousers, undies and socks that in the end we've kept him in
pull-ups...*

Memo to the writers: look, if your readers have children they will
have been through all this and have no wish to experience it again,
even second-hand. If they don't have children, they will find it
merely distasteful and quite likely to put them off their breakfast.

One sad thing is reading about children who have not turned
out how their parents might have wished. You just know that ten
years earlier their astonishing scholastic successes and sporting triumphs were blazoned all over the family newsletter. It is rather
different now.

ALLIE *decided that she wanted to go to study health and beauty
but would have to wait for another year to enrol for the course, so
we told her we would NOT be financing her to sit on her backside
doing nothing and hanging around with the (same, awful)
boyfriend. So she is currently working for an agency doing
office/computing work. She also works at a posh restaurant
greeting people at the door, once a week, and on Sundays she works
for a finance company dealing with telephone sales. We are still
trying to get her to pay for her keep, but haven't managed to come
up with a suitable arrangement yet! She told us a few days ago that
she is now considering joining the Police Force. She is also dating*

other boys as well as the (awful current) boyfriend. Watch this space!

RODDY *is twenty-two already, but still finding his way in life. He's living at home, but not interacting much with us. He spends his time making music (drum and bass, electronica), fishing, hanging out with his mates and having a good time, all of which is OK, but he's got no job, no money, no goals, limited options, and gives his parents grave concern.*

JAMES *is doing very well at school, and appears to be ahead in development compared to Geoffrey at a similar age. Geoffrey is doing equally well, and his teacher is very pleased with his progress thus far. Jill is of the opinion that he is of average ability, unlike John.*

Some are positively runic.

KEVIN *continues to be Kevin.*

What can that possibly convey to anyone who doesn't know Kevin? Finally, the fact that most round robin writers assume that their readers are as intrigued by their children as they are can lead them to produce the most astonishing lists of offspring and other relations — often without even the faintest hint about who they are or even how old they might be.

FAMILY *news? Aelred is enjoying training to be a magistrate, while*

Cassie does Citizens' Advice Bureau work; Roger has switched careers and is back at Oxford training to teach German; Dr Bill (Ph.D) is lecturing in German also in Oxford. Ailish, still part time at the Special Needs school, is dearly loved by the teenagers; Crispin does extra mural police work in London; Cordelia (Hons degree, Warwick) has also switched tracks and is training to teach ballet, Araminta continues with top grades in Classics at London Uni; Roberta continues to make her own stunning 'designer' clothes for a hobby (wish I was her size, for discards!), Lettice studying Construction Engineering / planning at Nottingham Trent Uni; Henrietta reading psychology at Swansea and spending most of her spare time with Army TA activities; Millie continues to hold down demanding jobs in the office and with the family; Simeon graduated from Leeds and is having a gap year, in Leeds, Tom is following Music interests – hoping eventually to be in a group – Rose also having gap year from Art college; Stu, now thirteen, greatly enjoying his drum kit. Hope the neighbours appreciate his style!

The recipient of that letter writes: 'We have not met any of their children, except Roger, who was very strange.'

The Sin of Smug Self-Satisfaction

IF THERE IS one thing that enrages the recipients of Christmas newsletters as much as perfect children, it's self-congratulation, smugness and the unspoken theme of the letter: don't you wish you were us? The message that oozes off the page seems to be 'our lives are quite, quite wonderful. How about yours?' To people who live in a small urban flat and have a forty-minute commute to a dreary job, whose annual holiday may be two weeks in a damp Welsh cottage, and whose homes are packed with wobbly furniture from Ikea and moribund beanbags, these golden, privileged lives are infuriating.

Holidays are probably the worst. Some people do little else than go on vacation, and like to list all their trips in exhaustive detail.

> HIGHLIGHTS *of my tours were the antiques safaris to Ireland, but every trip had its moments! Eurostar to Paris started the year where the agricultural show is always high on my list... with free wine tasting, and a lunch of oysters, mussels, sauerkraut, Limousin steaks, it is always great fun.*

Then it's Paris again in March, and Amiens in April.

Costa brava for a boys' week was as enjoyable as ever. Tom appointed me chainsaw expert to cut down overgrown bougainvilleas, etc. The reward was a side trip to Andorra, trips in the power boat, and superb food in local restaurants... Galloway in western Ireland was an extremely interesting trip in May. It was the first time I had been to this part of Ireland, a bit wild and woolly but super people and wonderful scenery... in Dordogne at Whit weekend we hired a local guide to see this lovely area of France. The village of Aradour sur Glane was an eye-opener. Look it up on the internet!

We will!

Next they're off to Holland, where they visit a wind generator, which supplies electricity to the grid and, we learn, gives an excellent return on money invested. Then it's Lyons, for a culture tour and a four-hour lunch with the Beekeepers Society. Lille follows ('a huge success'), then the Wye Valley, and a trip to Champagne where they buy the local tipple 'at under £7 a bottle'.

Ecuador and Galapagos was the final fling of the year!... The cruise went very quickly with quite hot weather, animals and birds that one could almost stroke, treks on islands, the crew diving for delicious lobsters in crystal clear water and of course the visit to see lonely George the tortoise... the jungle experience was different! Not as hot and humid as I expected but very nice people and a plant-person's paradise...

At this point, the average reader will cast the letter aside with a weary sigh and wonder if that B&B in Margate has been booked up for August yet.

These people in east London seamlessly blend their hectic charity work with their equally hectic travels:

> IN ADDITION, *we have managed the usual assortment of activities — plant sale in May raising £15,000 for local charities, hospice garden party in June, parish weekend in June, Tom to Canada on a Rotary fellowship exchange in July (with an additional week to visit friends in Ontario, including Pat's Mum and Dad), a 'Bolivia Bonanza' again in October, which raised £5,050 for Lucy and Pat's work in Bolivia — after which we enjoyed a 'rest' for a week in Tunisia, seeing Roman remains and experiencing Ramadan! In the background has been the GP practice for Tom, event planning and gardening for Jenny, St John's Ambulance, church, Rotary, and DIY for Tom! As soon as Jenny gets back from Bolivia, we'll be into the mad rush of Christmas preparation activities, Christmas day with Amanda and Art at Field Cottage, Boxing Day party here, before we fly out for a cruise from Mahé to Singapore! (To get our strength up for another year of exciting activities and visitors!)*

Just reading about it induces a terrible sense of malaise in the recipient. Other people are less inclined to force their travels down your throat, and focus quickly on the truly intriguing details:

ALAN *has traveled extensively this year, most recently to Azad*
Kashmir. In a bazaar in Muzzaffarabad, he met a bloke from
Bradford.

Nothing more is said about the bloke, or what he was doing away
from Bradford. However, it's amazing who you do meet.

WE ALL *took off for Palm Springs for the guys to play golf. Staying*
at La Quinta, a favourite haunt of movie stars in the 30s and 40s,
was quite a treat, an oasis of green with palms, orange and
grapefruit trees against a stunning backdrop of barren hills. Bright
blue skies with temperatures in the low 70s, but cool at night,
provided an invigorating environment... the icing on the cake was
undoubtedly when Tiger Woods brushed past our table as we were
sipping margaritas!

Brushes with the famous are not always mentioned with such
wide-eyed enthusiasm:

IN MARCH *we went to see Judi Dench in* All's Well That Ends
Well *in London, and were invited back to the Dame's dressing*
room for champagne afterwards — which was good fun, as always.

This next letter comes from people whose lives seem to be one
long round of fabulous trips and memorable occasions. They even
tell us all about the holidays they haven't been on yet:

WE'VE *just booked the first leg of a holiday for January 2006 — a twelve-day horse ride across the Torres del Paine national park in Patagonia (though we confess we are not camping), a voyage to Cape Horn (admittedly in a fair degree of luxury – no single-handed yachts for us) – followed by a leisurely amble by bus through Chile to the Atacama desert for a second ride. The travel agent emailed back to say: 'Wow!' We are planning ahead, aren't we! And as that is a long way off, we are also planning a shorter camping trip to Oman in March.*

Then their daughter gets married, and the ceremony is – unsurprisingly – not only perfect but also full of crazy, 'off the wall' humour:

The ceremony took place as planned in Yorkshire and the Gods smiled upon us. It was the most perfect day of the entire summer – warm, blue sky, no wind and an idyllic setting… the ceremony was punctuated by a series of readings – notably Hiawatha, The Owl and the Pussy Cat, and other similarly highbrow material. Much video was taken – including a most pleasing close-up shot of a guest surreptitiously removing her shoes, which evidently were pinching badly.

That happened six months before they wrote the letter. Not only can they still remember that one of the guests had tight-fitting shoes, they also feel the need to tell their friends about this riveting detail:

... Then to dinner, beautifully served in the ancient dining room with portraits, darkened by time and smoke, of Yorkshire heroes from a bygone age – Boycott, Trueman, Hutton – sorry, only joking! Speeches of course, preceded by gagging orders handed down by the bride with threats of High Court actions if certain past deeds were exposed...

(At this point, I must insert news of another wedding, this time in the Midlands:

A LOVELY event was the marriage in July of Iain and Megan, his partner of some eleven years. They did the legal bit at the Register Office, but the 'real' ceremony was in their garden, where there was a grand marquee, caterers, dancers, musicians, and flowers. The theme was a cruise ship in the 1920s, and no detail was missed. The marriage, conducted by the ship's captain, of course, included poems and speeches, and an exchange of vows which had been decided on by Iain and Megan themselves. Later, Megan donned her clog dancing costume, and performed with her clog-morris team.

You can, I fear, almost hear the stifled giggles emitted by the inebriated guests at this point.)

Back to the family whose daughter married in Yorkshire. They barely pause for breath.

As soon as the wedding was over and the bills paid, we embarked on a four-week visit to Malawi and South Africa...

Here they visit game parks, find a six-inch locust in their bedroom, contemplate buying a tract of land in the Karoo desert, and discover how whites in the new South Africa have adapted to the end of apartheid.

> *And then, finally, by train to visit more old friends and colleagues in Johannesburg, Pretoria and Tzaneen, before returning home. We are making a short repeat visit to Cape Town, mainly for academic purposes, in January. It's a hard life.*
>
> *In spite of our continuing fascination with Africa, Sheffield has plenty of compensations…*

This great city seems to have a powerful fascination for some round-robiners:

> SANDRA *and Archie continue with their Life of Riley. They took the two boys to Egypt over the New Year and topped that by taking them to Peru in April. Cuzco, Arequipa, Lake Titicata, Machu Picchu and a flight over the Nasca lines to boot. They drove over a pass 4,500 metres high to reach the lake. On their own they have had a holiday in Croatia and liked it so much that they bought a holiday home there. In addition they have started to buy a home in Sheffield.*

Some people, perhaps not being acquainted with the delights and the fleshpots of Sheffield, insist on going abroad anyway:

> OUR FIRST *holiday was in February when we went on a three-*

week 'Volcano trek' in Tanzania, with the main aim of climbing Mt.
Kilimanjaro. We climbed three other volcanoes first and saw two
safari parks, so it was very varied… on the summit of Kilimanjaro
I have never been so cold in all my life: -10°C, with a howling gale
off the glacier. I resolved never to climb another mountain ever
again, but this is already weakening… since it had been my idea to
climb Kili, Dennis chose our next holiday destination, Afghanistan.
We went in August with the same tour leader who had taken us to
pre-war Iraq.

They see wonderful sights: mosques, the site where the Taliban
blew up the giant Buddhas, and the 800-year-old minaret of Djam,
which stands isolated in a deep, rocky gorge.

It was exciting getting there, as we thought our minibus driver had
done a runner while we were walking the gorge, with all our
luggage, money and passports (just a misunderstanding in the end).
Then we had to wade a fast flowing river, several of the party fell
in, ruining cameras etc. Further on we learned that our only road
was blocked by a battle between the armies of two local warlords.
Fortunately the warlords very courteously agreed to stop fighting
for a while to let us through, and duly did so!

The reader at this point wants to say that he, for one, quite likes
Torquay at this time of year. But our writer's travels are not finished.

Our last holiday was in October when we borrowed Jason and Daph's holiday bungalow in the Lake District near Penrith. We stayed with them in Manchester on our way up there, which was lovely, and then had three glorious autumn days. It wasn't quite as testing as Kili, but we put in quite hard treks and certainly set a faster pace than we had been allowed in Tanzania.

Of course, on the other hand, some people have already seen it all:

So I HAD Jim's full support when I declared I wanted to go with Denise. The deal was that I would go with her to Machu Picchu (which was not high on my list of priorities, as I had been there twice before).

This is from a couple who live at a very expensive address in the Middle East:

WE NOW split our time four ways: Devon, Cobham, Dubai and our yacht, Aloha (now being refitted for our retirement voyages). Just at the time I was savouring visions of a simpler life, it has now just ramped up in complexity!

They buy a new Range Rover, to complement the one they have in Dubai. She puts a Mini-Cooper S convertible on order. Their daughter gets a first-class degree, and becomes engaged to a man who proposed on the top floor of a seven-star hotel in Dubai. They also have a granddaughter:

She truly is the sunniest, cuddliest little girl there ever could be! I
was slobbered with kisses tonight – hair and forehead duly covered
in a yoghurty, fruity fool!

How tempted we may be to join the little girl in covering them with yoghurty slobber! Soon they are off again on their travels:

The Big Trip was a diversion: encompassing, variously, northern
Spain, London, Brisbane briefly, a long time in Fiji, ditto Vanuatu,
New South Wales and Perth. Much of this time was spent with
people very dear to us. In Spain we attended José and Gemma's
wedding in Zaragoza. In Fiji we joined Sven and Eleanor on board
Romantica, *their catamaran, finally crossing with them to*
Vanuatu… whilst I was in New Zealand, Stanley visited François
and Janie Vorsteen in Islamabad. It was an opportunity for
marvellous sight-seeing into the furthermost reaches of Pakistan…
perhaps we will catch up with you in one place or another!

Not if we can help it, I suspect.

Some people long for you to know just how many homes they possess. This letter, ostensibly from a mere suburb of south London, ends:

Do *come and visit us, in London, Paris, Saltaire, or Boston!*

Others imply that the many travels on which their wealth takes them are in fact closer to spiritual journeys than the package tours most people opt for.

> 'OH, WOW!' *is an expression frequently on the lips of Veronica (now ten). Her life is packed full with wonder: 'When I grow up I want to travel round the world, become an explorer, go scuba diving, study animals, go to the moon, become a detective, study dreams, swim with whales and study ghosts.' She and Jack (eight) help to keep alive in us a sense of wonder.*
>
> *Looking back on the year, we are inclined to say 'Wow' on account of the richness of experience it has brought. Some examples: Monteverdi Vespers in Wells Cathedral; finding fritillaries flowering in a mediaeval cloister in... New York; discussing metaphysics under the stars in July with our next-door neighbours after their Buddhist wedding celebration; P. being present at the birth in August of a much longed-for child for our friends Ginny and Rod (former Fr. Mick of the University chaplaincy); walking our last stretch of the Dorset coast path in evening summer sunshine; picking sloes with our cousins against a blue sky and golden leaves background... those tastes constitute the hors d'oeuvre of this year's Christmas letter. Now for the main course:*

Er, no, thanks, I really am full already. In fact I ought to be getting home in time for, um, *Celebrity Big Brother*...

Here is another family that just can't stay still for more than a few days:

No sooner *had we moved in, when Jilly flew off with her girlfriends to Megève in France, for a week's skiing... February: Ivor (with the lads!) was lucky enough (again) to go skiing, for the second year running to Courchevel. Later we visited Poole in Dorset, for a long weekend. It is a remarkable area and was recently cited as one of the three most expensive pieces of real estate in the world! It was lovely, but in price terms was maybe a little over-rated, in our view!*

March finds them in France with two other couples, then in April they have a craft weekend in Devon.

May: Jilly joined a group of girls in Barcelona on a hen trip, and Ivor went with 'the lads' on a pre-arranged stag trip to Prague where they had a splendid time including whitewater rafting, go-karting and shooting...

Not the reasons why most people go to Prague, but then there is no accounting for tastes.

June: Ivor's sister Angela celebrated her fiftieth birthday!! A whole week of festivities ensued, and Angela decided to live out her fantasy of being the Lady of the Manor, and hired a real one in the Cotswolds for the weekend.

Come July, and they are at Hever Castle for a jazz festival, and later in the month they are back in France 'for golf and merriment'. Their son goes on an activity holiday in Kent. In August it's back to France for 'two fantastic weeks' involving barbecues and an impromptu guitar concert with their Belgian neighbour. It is the last of eleven holidays they have had between them.

Some people feel that their trips can only be shared and relished if they are described in quite pitiless detail. These people live near London, and the recipient of their letter has helpfully counted up seven holidays in the course of the year, beginning with Naples, continuing on their canal boat, *Eagle's Nest*, then a ride on the Eurostar to Paris where they pass on a useful tip. When on a *bateau mouche*:

> IT PAYS *to dine at a table for two — the wines are advertised as 'one bottle between three' with each course. Which meant we got two bottles between two!!!*

Then their son and daughter-in-law arrange a vast and incredibly complex holiday in Canada.

> *Why complex? Well, I'll explain. There were seven of us spending our holiday in Canada, Cathy and I; Emily; Steve and Tasha — and Scott and Eva. No, we're not all travelling together; that would be just too simple. S & T flew out on the 3rd to Calgary, where they spent two nights before hiring a camper van to explore the Rockies ... all except S & T flew into Edmonton on 7 July, not direct as*

planned, but diverted to Vancouver where we had a three-hour wait
for a connecting internal flight back over the Rockies to Edmonton.
Whilst in Vancouver airport, we met up with cousins Grant and Sue
on Grant's day off from his job — at Vancouver airport!

Soon afterwards, things get really complicated. They go to an
island off the coast of British Columbia:

Our stay on the island was magical — Scott and Eva, Cathy and I
shared a house next door to cousins Anna and Edward, while S & T
became 'trailer trash' with Emily in the huge mobile home on the
next plot. Over the next few days, we met just about everyone on the
island and spent many happy hours with Louis and Jo, Anna and
Edward, Andrew and Colette, Vicky, Randy and Berthilde and all
those super kids. It was especially good to see Randy for one last
time.

Why? Where is he going? Does he have a fatal disease?

... Each morning we awoke to find deer roaming the gardens
and each evening we're back round for another family gathering.
All too soon, we're bidding farewell and taking the Monday
morning ferry back, then onward to Horseshoe Bay for the short
drive into Vancouver City for our last two nights in Canada. That
evening we all met up with cousins Di, Kitty, Kirk, Bobbie and
Charles for a splendid Chinese meal. S & T, S & E, had chosen a
downtown hotel to be close to the nightlife, while we were the other

end of Robson Street, within walking distance of Stanley Park. On our final night we had dinner with...

At this point we pray: no more names. We didn't know any of these people anyway. But we are not yet out of the woods.

... Max, and his kids Tiggie and Ben, with whom we abandoned Emily. She spent another five weeks with Max and Charlotte and the kids in Vancouver and returned just in time to collect her GCSE results. I'm banned from telling you what they were...

Though I think we can guess.

... But let's just say that we were very impressed.

Here's another family that wants to share every single moment of their travels with us:

FORGET PALIN, *we have been living a life of fast and furious adventures!!!* Bridget Jones's Diary *is no match for our journal. Check out the highlights below...*

March. Having had a great Christmas in Australia we have come back with lobster patches... managed to transport back ten bottles of wine from the Barossa in hand baggage, no mean feat... decide to recreate the holiday feeling with a couple of weekends away in Cornwall. Tim and I have now been together for ten years... he has learned to enjoy EastEnders *and* Coronation Street *and we own a leaf shredder.*

We have had ten great years of love and friendship, lots of exciting adventures, and only two serious rows – a significant achievement.

April:Tim, Mum and I go on holiday to Russia with love for a week.

But the airline loses their baggage, and Mum has to go round St Petersburg in trainers and a T-shirt.

It's May now, and they are off on a trip to Derbyshire. Sadly, raw sewage bubbles up through the flooring of the bathroom in their holiday cottage. Next month, they are back north at Robin Hood's Bay. They contemplate moving to Whitby, but recall this is where Dracula made landfall in Bram Stoker's novel, and they decide that too many of the locals look like vampires. No holiday for the next three months because they're moving house. But:

October:Tim and I take passage to India.

Here, like so many Europeans, they find the experience spiritually enlightening, at least part of the time:

India is a fantastic country, with so much to see and learn, but, wow, there are some very, very bad smells.

This next letter proves that nothing, absolutely nothing, will keep our newsletter writers from their travels. It recounts no fewer than eighteen trips, all taken during what must have been a remarkably hectic twelve months.

An EVENTFUL year! Our first grandchild, Dylan John, arrived on April 22nd, David was elevated to the peerage as a working peer, and I was diagnosed with a rare breast cancer, had surgery in July, finished radiotherapy in November, and now await the reconstruction route! Otherwise life went on as before.

The trips are endless: a conference in Reading, followed by an annual visit to Spain, then a weekend in Washington DC. There are three weekends in Berlin, visiting their son's partner, and there's their annual trip up the Thames in their own boat. They take her mother to the Channel Islands, and visit Wales. They go to historic car races, and David still flies a plane.

I taught at the University of Malta at the end of January and visited the University of North Carolina in March for a Ph.D. student's defence...

What he or she needed defending from is not explained.

... To Atlanta for the USA Science Teachers' conference in April followed by another conference in Cyprus. I also attended the American Museum conference in New Orleans in May and returned in September for the American Zoo conference. I took a nostalgic trip to Hong Kong in September for the International Zoo Educators' conference and managed to visit a few old haunts. At the end of July I had a therapeutic visit to New York for the Conservation Biology conference and saw friends and several

> *museums, art galleries, and zoos too! I went to Woburn for the UK*
> *Zoo Federation conference in November and then to Seattle for a*
> *science teachers' conference. We had a week in Antigua at the*
> *beginning of October…*

This from someone who is undergoing surgery for breast cancer! One can only stand back in awed admiration.

Not everybody's travels are quite as successful. There is an interesting sub-genre of letters written by people who have decidedly crummy holidays:

> OUR HOLIDAY *in Cornwall was a bit of a washout. It rained*
> *almost every day, the cottage leaked and we got little help from the*
> *owner, a grumpy farmer who appeared to object to us parking our*
> *car anywhere, even though he had acres of what seemed to be empty*
> *land. Television reception was fuzzy, to say the least, and when we*
> *tried out the Scrabble set we found it had several letters missing. We*
> *were reduced to buying a pack of cards at a petrol station…*
> *wishing you everything we would wish for ourselves in 2005.*

These people have another problem – international one-upmanship:

> BOTH DANIEL *and Tessa have been on exchange trips to Germany*
> *– Daniel to Munich, and Tessa to Düsseldorf; in return we have had*
> *three different German teenagers staying here, which has been*
> *rather daunting. Whereas D &T were taken off to various fests and*

*enjoyed the many and varied aspects of German culture, the best
our grammar school could drum up was Cadbury's World and a
Victorian pumping station. We did our best to compensate at
weekends, but we were badly let down by the weather each time, and
our beach picnics had to be cancelled. Try as we might, we found it
impossible to prance around in national costume doing pretty
dances, so we couldn't help but feel inadequate!*

There should be a name for it: EVI, or Exchange Visit Inadequacy.
Agencies would promise to solve the problem. For only £2,000 a
head you could give your teenage visitor tickets for the men's final
at Wimbledon, a Coldplay concert, and dinner at Gordon
Ramsay's.

As it happens, pumping stations may be boring for German
youth, but not for everyone. This letter is from the West Country:

EARLIER *in the year we had a week in Andalusia, where Liz was
delighted by the wealth of wild flowers and Frank was fascinated by
the nearby pumped storage electricity system, so fun for all!*

One reader sent in four letters from an old university friend:

I HAVE *been receiving these for over twenty years now, and began to
keep them when I realised that much of the perverse delight of
receiving each year's letter lay in its similarity to the year before,
building up a cumulative picture of a life of quiet monotony
punctuated by small disappointments.*

The woman whose life is described in these letters travels a great deal, but nowhere she goes ever quite lives up to expectations.

SALZBURG in Austria was lovely, unfortunately we only had a half a day there, so we couldn't see it properly.

Munich was nice, modern, but not too much so, workmanlike, rather like Manchester or Birmingham, rather than romantic, like Rome, Venice or Florence. I didn't like the Italian cities much, though, they were a bit scruffy.

I sent some pictures to Amateur Photographer, some months ago, and had high hopes of their being accepted, as the magazine hung on to them for quite a while, but they didn't get used in the end.

I went to London with Aunt Phyllis. We stayed in a little hotel in Wembley, which it took ages for me to find, since I couldn't find the street it was on and no one, but no one, I asked had a clue. I think the locals must all go round with their eyes shut.

Prague, where we finished up, is beautiful. Parts of it are like Glasgow, though the main bits aren't.

She goes to a school reunion where she poses for a group photograph:

It took two attempts for my copy to be delivered — the first time, the photo wasn't in the envelope. As it had to be signed for, I had to get up and answer the door to the postman, two times in a row!

She has an eerie knack of being in a place but missing the point of it:

We also visited Monaco, where we stayed for about three hours. It was quite interesting, but nothing to rave about. We did see the outside of the Casino, with all the Rolls-Royces parked outside, but didn't go in.

In Salamanca, some of my friends went to a bullfight, but I didn't.

In July I went over to Edinburgh for the official opening of the Parliament. I was quite near the (temporary) accommodation the Parliament is in, and I saw a lot of the processions going in, but, being outside, heard nothing of the proceedings inside. I should have taken a radio over. There was a screening of the ceremonies in Princes Street Gardens, but that was not where I was.

Some people have a habit of bringing you up sharply and uncomfortably, like finding a ball bearing in a chocolate whip. This letter is from Hampshire:

Our 'big' holiday this year was in California in October; they'd had no rain at all for six months until we arrived, and apart from seeing a fatal crash at the San Diego airshow, we had a good time shopping, sightseeing and splashing round in swimming pools.

Or:

> AT THE END *of the month Ray went to a week's dig at Syon Abbey, in the footprints of the Time Team, which was very interesting, but a bit disconcerting when he dug up some human remains.*

> NANCY *finished in June her degree at Leicester, and then went on a three-month trip to Kyrgyzstan, Tibet, China, ending in Nepal where Maoist rebels endeavoured to squeeze a ransom from her of $50, which she negotiated down to $25.*

These people would have a better time if they didn't have to share their personal space quite so much:

> FEBRUARY *saw our annual skiing trip to France, and the fun started with the train journey to Stansted. Our carriage contained a skinhead nutter, cackling and muttering maniacally. Many people avoided eye contact, but Alex befriended him by doing impressions of various cartoon characters, which thankfully made him laugh hysterically and be our mate, instead of slaying us with a meat cleaver… during the summer we had a few days away at a holiday park in Devon, where most of our fellow holiday-makers seemed to have tattoos, broken teeth and noses, and cauliflower ears. And that was just the women!*

Whereas these people apologize for writing at all.

> IN SPITE *of all the snide comments about silly Christmas letters,*

you get that or just a signature. Clara's sister Jean died just before
Christmas...

They plough onwards anyway. They go for a holiday in the Alps, and enjoy some magnificent scenery:

The next stop was in the Parc National de la Vanoise. It is a local
market town as well as a resort, so it is a pleasant spot with a good
campsite. Unfortunately the weather started getting a bit unsettled
at this point, though Jim got in one short and one longer walk. The
main entertainment was the toilet door saga. Georgia finds the
'squatters' very difficult on account of her arthritic ankles, so was
disconcerted when the handle came off the door of the only 'sitter',
leaving it unlocked or locking oneself in. A couple of kids got locked
in, and then the door disappeared completely. Good thing I'm not
bashful. Eventually they transplanted a door from the adjacent
'squatter'...

And so on. The tale occupies roughly twice as much space as Jean's death.

The wife in this letter takes a holiday in Poland with a friend, leaving her husband behind with his two prolapsed discs.

WE STAYED in Cracow. Such lovely gentle and polite people. One
of our days was spent at Auschwitz, a very moving experience,
although not as grim as it must have been in the depths of winter.
We were fortunate to have blue sky and sun, and the trees the

prisoners had planted were tall and green, giving the impression of
a rather pleasant council estate.

Strange how few people return from Auschwitz with that particular impression.

But then everywhere has its disappointments. Our round-robinners are, as ever, undaunted:

OUR BIG *trip this summer was to Hungary. We decided to drive*
there. It's just 1,300 miles there (and 1,300 miles back!). We
rented a house on the shore of Lake Balaton for two weeks; this is a
freshwater lake about fifty miles long. The location was very
picturesque, the weather was absolutely fantastic, and the water
temperature around 75°F. The only downside was the food and
drink, even though we managed to find Tesco's... the only mishap
occurred ten miles from home, when a young lad came flying out of
a side road and ran into the wheel arch of the car. Sod's Law!
Actually that was the second of three accidents in Derek's BMW.
The first happened in a car park, someone backed into him while he
was stationary, the third came ten days after he had got the car
back from the second prang, when a chap drove into the back of him
at a junction in town. So the poor old car has had a new rear end
three times, all at someone else's expense, fortunately.

Do the writers imagine that we actually care about the minor bumps and scrapes they have? Months after they happened?

These people take a holiday in Kenya:

WE PILED *our kit into the Land Rover and took off across the*
Laikipia Plain to the exquisitely majestic Matthews Mountains. As
soon as we arrived in camp, a scorpion lurking in Harry's towel
stung him on the hand. He yelled. His hand was on fire. A fine-
boned Samburu girl called Helena ran to his aid. In forty-minute
sessions three times a day she worked her Nilotic magic on his arm.
She muttered incantations, spat and worked his flesh in rough rings
of deep massage, working in her saliva and a greasy herbal
embrocation...

Enough already! We are pleased to learn that Harry gets better
soon, but, having fallen for the lovely, deliciously slobbering
Helena, 'spent the rest of the week hoping to be stung again'.

For the most part, our writers' trips abroad are triumphant successes. Still, not all complacent, nerve-grinding, tooth-furring
smugness concerns holidays, though it can seem that way. Some
people manage to be pleased with themselves about almost anything;

As I *write, Camilla's powder-blue BMW sits in the driveway below*
my window...

These people begin by describing something that happened more
than a year ago, merely because they forgot to mention it in their
previous newsletter:

USUALLY *after sending out our Norton News, we realize that we have missed off something most important — and this was the case last year. We completely forgot to mention what must have been the highlight of last year — being among the winners in the ballot for seats to attend the Three Tenors Concert in Bath...*

Some people just have a strange sense of priorities. These people live in the Home Counties, and are clearly well-off, a fact which they manage to imply fairly often:

I NEVER *really saw the need to own a swimming pool, but I have to say that, like central heating and dishwashers, they do rather win you round once you have them...*

They take their holidays in Australia:

It was ludicrously good. Day after day of clear blue skies, fantastic and fabulously diverse scenery, and people who are great fun but immensely helpful and practical. Heron Island, a coral cay 70 km off the Pacific coast, is simply one of the most beautiful places any of us have ever been. Thousands of birds, millions of fish, baby turtles scuttling into the sea, and sharks which are big enough to boast about but small enough not to eat you in one mouthful. In Sydney we cadged splendid lunches off Jack and Hilary, and Bruce and Denise, though we realized halfway round that we had completely missed out Melbourne. Sorry, Geoff, we must catch up in the New Year.

Then, and only then (after a brief description of the disappointing progress being made by the builders working on their house), does the writer mention the fact that his wife had to have an emergency heart operation — 'tomorrow!' said her GP. Luckily she recovers.

> *Sophie had her ninth birthday at the end of May, by which time Delia was well enough to create an elaborate cake. Sophie is an excellent swimmer and inevitably decided she wanted a pool party. One good thing about spending thousands on renovating a swimming pool is that it saves you a few quid each year in trips to bowling alleys and soft play centers. I see it as an investment...*

Our round-robiners are rarely still:

> THIS PRETTY *much sums up our lives these days: far too much to do and never enough time. As if horses, cats, fish, estate management (large-scale) holiday lettings, mega DIY and the usual work and study were not enough, the beginning of 2004 brought us a new business challenge... we finally did clear out and set up our display room for our ever-growing ceramics collection. What did we do before eBay? (Apart from sleep occasionally).*

These next people lead lives of unremitting self-congratulation. They decide to move from a village in East Anglia to a market town:

WE WERE *lucky to find just what we wanted, and moved in June. The house is an early Victorian town house in Georgian style, recently restored to a very high standard.*

The estate agents may have seen them coming...

There is a patio garden (no more mowing!) that opens directly through wrought iron gates onto the Great Churchyard. From our main guestroom on the top floor, one can see the Cathedral, the historic Norman tower, St Tabitha's church and the brewery — what a location!

Dealing with a quarter century's worth of accumulated junk and coping with all the stresses of moving took a lot of time, but we still found the energy to do some travelling (during the year Will flew the Atlantic twelve times and Jessica ten times).

These folk have a lot of New Age beliefs, shared by their pregnant daughter and her fiancé.

THEY ARE *contemplating tying the knot with a handfasting ceremony in line with their Celtic beliefs. They exchange solstice presents — homeopathic birthing kit, eco nappies, stretchmark cream, books for the New Age* (Parenting Post 9/11, The Oxford Dictionary of 10,000 Names, Let Birth Be Born Again). *Tamsin is one of only two mothers preparing for a home birth in the whole of Leeds!*

Sometimes an apparently normal letter brings you up short with one smug line:

> TOBY *has settled into what was Reading's first nuclear-free street.*

Or a smug paragraph:

> THERE'S *no place like home — especially when it has a retracting downdraft extractor fan, induction hob, steam room, marble-topped underfloor heating, and, best of all, a purpose-built, seven-speaker surround-sound home cinema with eight-foot screen and two-tier seating...*

This fellow has become mayor of the small West Country market town in which he and his wife live. She can't get over the excitement:

> WHAT A YEAR *we have had! Paul was inaugurated Mayor in May, and since then the time has simply flown by. As Mayor, he automatically becomes chairman of several organizations in town, and honorary member of several others. He attends many meetings as town councillor and as Mayor. I just have to attend to the social side, and have finally discovered the meaning of the term 'social whirl'. As Mayoress, I have to look the part, so I have the perfect excuse for lots of retail therapy (when I have time).*
>
> *On civic occasions only, Paul wears robes and we both wear our chains. On other, less formal, occasions, we wear our medallions*

which detach from the chains. The chains are all gold, and worth
thousands of pounds, so we are escorted by two Mace Bearers
and/or the Town Clerk and Mayors Cadet. Talk about Lord and
Lady Muck!

We've been wined and dined by most of the big organizations in
town, and by other mayors in the south-west, including the Lord
Mayor of Plymouth, and shaken hands with Lords and Ladies, TV
and radio personalities, and (Paul only) Prince Charles. I keep
expecting to wake up any minute to find it is all a dream… we
were driven in the parade through the town centre, and more
recently shared Santa's sleigh during our Edwardian evening. What
a learning curve this has been for us, and we still have five months
to go.

The next letter is almost 3,000 words long, and appears to contain
the complete record of the year for one highly achieving family.
The wife is no mere helpmeet, but 'the lynchpin that holds our
diversity together'. They are involved in motor racing, museums,
conservation, the Church, the Girl Guides, ballet, East European
development, and they have a cousin who is knighted for his stem
cell research. The children spend, so far as one can see, almost the
entire year travelling. This is the elder son:

In recent years, I have not been one to leave my rucksack in the
cupboard for long, and memorable trips this year have included a
lovely Easter break with Mum, Dad and Rebecca to Kaliningrad; a

fascinating journey through Ukraine with Vilnius friend Kiki; an
expedition with Stephen and Rebecca down to the Bialowieża
Forest in Poland, a visit to Minsk and to the Basovischa Belarusian
rock music festival in Poland in a forest near the Belarusian border;
and several meet-ups in the Baltic states and in Kaliningrad with
colleagues from other EC delegations in the region. I haven't
forgotten to go home either, including as usual for the British
Grand Prix...

But he appears to be a dull stay-at-home stick-in-the-mud compared to his adventurous sister Rebecca:

This year I have set foot in eighteen countries, changed hemisphere
four times, and I'm embarrassed to say I can still only converse in
one language! Off and on since March last year I have made
Lithuania my home... so where do the other seventeen countries fit
in? Well, I was in Ecuador for Christmas, Peru for the New Year,
travelled on through Bolivia, returned to Canada (via America) for
a few days snow-boarding in Whistler on my way home, before first
coming here to Lithuania. In March and April I made trips to
Belarus, Kaliningrad, Latvia and Estonia, before back home via
Denmark for two friends' weddings in May. Then a couple of weeks
at home in June before heading off for a month (via Singapore) in
Western Australia (a week down south, a week up north in Broome,
and then a tour back down to Perth again for a few more days). So
then to get back here again I went racing with Dad and Mum in

Holland via France and Belgium, and finally Dougal and I had a trip down to a Polish forest when Stephen came to visit. If any of you fancy an insight, we are having a cherry festival here in July 2005! And if you are ever in need, I now knit woolly hats and socks to order!

The younger son, Stephen, is an artist, but not just any old artist. He is a multimedia artist, pushing at the boundaries of the avant-garde:

Earlier this summer, I wrote of myself: 'Stephen Tomelty is an artist whose field of practice extends from performance to architecture and curating and from multimedia installations to interventions in the urban environment. Exploring the realm of relationships, he consistently engages in work that crosses the fault lines of media and disciplines.'... I always said that going on that course at the RCA was like going abroad to learn more about my own country. But, as with many journeys into foreign lands, it doesn't always fulfil your expectations... But I have become conversant in new languages. The question, as always in travelling, is: am I still the same person, or have I been changed in the process?

Sorry, can't help you there, squire. But at least it makes a change from swimming pools and powder-blue BMWs.

The Iniquity of Intemperate Information

ENOUGH, enough, stop! is the cry from so many recipients of Christmas newsletters. People who in their daily social discourse may seem quite reasonable and respectful of others' feelings suddenly get a debilitating case of logorrhoea when they sit down in front of a computer. How else can we explain extracts such as this?

> GIFTS received this year have included a towel ring for the bathroom, a handsome set of table mats showing West Country buildings, several classical CDs, a pair of glass candlesticks and one of those curled metal things that expand for you to put books in. You don't see those much any more, and I suspect it came from a charity shop.

Fair enough, but then finding the perfect gift is often a problem:

> JEREMY brought me back a present he had bought at Toronto airport, in haste, when returning from his long weekend. It was a chunky metal bracelet. Unfortunately it was too small for me, so we now use it for poaching eggs.

People can often bring unwanted news of problems at work. This is part of a newsletter consisting of several pages; all packed with detailed information about the economics of farming. Imagine asking this fellow, 'how are things on the farm?', and having him answer in just under a thousand words, of which this is the merest, shortest, sample:

> SUPERMARKETS *are importing beef at 98p per kilo, landed, from countries that do not have our regulatory regimes, whereas Scottish carcasses are fetching 192p per kilo, but our finishers need 220p per kilo to be profitable.*

That letter ends: 'and if you're coming our way, do give us a call!' Or, on reflection, perhaps not.

Farmers do seem liable to be more fascinated with the details of their lives than the rest of us might be. This son of the soil reminds us of previous disquisitions on the topic of arable yields:

> LAST YEAR *I wrote that 'beans were also a disappointment at 4.6 tonnes per hectare'. This year they yielded a mere 4.1 tonnes per hectare, so we are even more gloomy. Yet their long-term average over a decade makes them preferable to peas, which is why we have dropped the latter completely. Once again we have used our own farm-saved seed which,* deo gratias, *still shows no signs of aschochyta.*

Another glimpse into the modern bucolic life:

> I HAVE *now passed over my semen customers in Sussex to a new rep,*

and have been given more customers, and a bigger area locally,
which is really good, and I have recently won a couple of big orders
such that I earn enough from selling semen to cover the cost of
Kieran's wages…

Having the builders in is, of course, an important and sometimes upsetting event in people's lives. Naturally it sticks in their minds. But that is no reason why it should stick in ours:

WE FINALLY *managed to find a plumber to do our bathroom, and*
in February the bath was removed and we had a lovely, big corner
shower fitted. The bath was only used once in a blue moon, so we
don't miss it. We have plans to replace the kitchen roof and then re-
do the whole kitchen layout next, but quite when that will get done
is another matter. Stephen wants to stick with a reliable builder we
know rather than try someone else, but as he is a one-man band, it
could be quite a while before he finishes other projects. In the
meantime I have arranged our little bedroom so that it is still a
bedroom…

Yes, of course. Can't you just get the stuff done then invite us round to admire it?

But farmers and home-improvers may not be quite as obsessed as IT specialists. This is the second paragraph of a letter from the south-east:

OUR *local grammar school set Stuart a couple of challenges for*

*the financial year which commenced on 1st April — to change the
provider of the payroll service (after the county council service
proved so awful month after month from September 2002) and to
change the DOS-based accounting software (which had served well
from 1994) for a Windows-based system. Thanks to careful
planning the new payroll provider has provided a vastly better
service at no greater cost, whilst the new accounting package does
offer some advantages, but at the expense of noticeably reduced
speed of operation…*

Or take this, the longest paragraph in one Christmas letter:

*IF YOU create a document in Word or Excel and then send it to
someone that does not have the relevant Word or Excel program,
they can download a free viewer from the MS website. You would
think Bill [Gates] could do the same for MS Publisher, since very
few people have that — I think you have to buy MS Office Pro
nowadays before that item is thrown in.*

Or:

*FOR your information, this newsletter is typed on a DECpc 425 I
Intel using the latest Word For Windows package… did I mention
that our old cat died after being with us for 18 years? She just got
thinner and thinner and then walked off. It was sad, we never found
the body, and the boys and I had meant to carry out an autopsy.*

For some people there is a degree of relish in describing what they are *not* doing. They draw quiet satisfaction from telling us how little is happening in their lives, though they often do so at considerable length.

JOHN, *Julian and I have survived 2003 without encountering any further radical disturbances in our lives during the course of the year. This is not to say that nothing has changed — far less that no progress has occurred — only that we are all still living in the same places and the same networks of relationships, and pursuing our labours with the same organizations as we were a year ago.*

In that case, one is tempted to yell, why are you bothering to write to us? Take this letter:

THIS *has not been a year of great excitement.*

That turns out to be a trifle unfair on the writers, who can at least inform us:

Recorder playing has taken a bit of a back seat this past year.

THINKING *about the past year there is not a great deal to tell you; at least not a great deal that would be of interest. I suppose it was quite dramatic a few days ago to receive a letter to tell me that my winter fuel allowance would be paid into my bank account within days...*

This writer is also being unfair on himself, for two paragraphs later:

> *I have had a recurrence of the problems with kidney stones…*
> *however, investigations have failed to locate any more stones. Either*
> *they are very small, or I may possibly have passed them.*

Another letter begins:

> NOTHING *major springs to mind for this year, so I could just say*
> *we're all a year older with a few more wrinkles, and sign off here.*
> *However, I have had one or two complimentary comments in the*
> *past about these newsletters which I do in fact enjoy doing, so will*
> *try and bring the day-to-day stuff to life. Maybe I could keep it to*
> *two pages this year! Joke.*

And a joke it turns out to be, since the letter is four pages of A4 paper. Writers should be able to distinguish between polite enthusiasm from their readers and genuine interest. For, as someone who can recall the past in detail, this woman does not exactly rival Marcel Proust:

> *3 Jan: Had our now sort of traditional turkey curry party.*
> *10 Jan: reciprocal Twelfth Night party at a neighbours'. Won the*
> *fun quiz, and got a plant, which shrivelled and died.*
> *29 Feb: watched Carling Cup final at Will's club. Middlesbrough*
> *won 2–1.*
> *23 Apr: Had to rescue Martin and Kate as Kate had managed to*

lock the keys in the car while they were getting the weekly fish and chips.
6 Jun: watched lots of v. moving things on TV about D-Day.
18 Jun: amazed to find Harrods is shut on Sundays.

Space does not permit me to quote from her trenchant strictures on Newcastle airport car park.

This is from a similarly chronological account of the year in northern Scotland:

JUNE: *Septic tank gets emptied.*

The retail experience clearly has a grip on many correspondents. Here is an Australian resident returning to his homeland:

ONE *anecdote: while posting a parcel, the assistant at the post office asked me how many pounds it was. My reply was along the lines of not knowing how much it weighed. As the assistant stared back, Amanda nudged me… cost! I've still got the English accent.*

Or:

WE MADE *several trips to Ikea in Birmingham. On one visit we managed to fit the lovely new dining table and chairs into the car, but not me and the girls! Mark had to make two round trips to Birmingham and to make the situation worse, he had got home with the table, only to find he couldn't get it in the house as I had the keys! (Just as well, he had his own set of garage keys.)*

The same letter reveals that the writer's car had a clutch problem.

> *The original one wore out in November 2002 and was replaced at*
> *'Mr Clutch'. Twelve months and 9,000 miles later it started*
> *slipping so Don took it back in November 2003. On examination,*
> *they said it was worn out, and was not covered by the warranty. He*
> *therefore had to pay for it to be replaced, despite protests that he*
> *had never had a clutch wear out in such a short time. In March*
> *2004 he took it back again as it was making a lot of noise and they*
> *had to replace the cover plate. After this, it started juddering…*

This saga goes on for quite a lot longer, offering even more car maintenance news than most of us might feel we strictly require. But then people seem to be endlessly fascinated by their own vehicles:

> IN APRIL *we said farewell after seven years to 'Monty', my diesel*
> *Mondeo, in favour of a silver Toyota Avensis with sports alloy*
> *wheels.*

> I SPLASHED *out and bought a new car, my first ever! And am*
> *delighted with it – a Skoda Fabia which averages about 55mpg,*
> *has low emissions, and is full of gizmos such as air conditioning,*
> *side air bags, and a cooled drinks compartment – and with turbo*
> *diesel injection, it goes pretty well too.*

In other words, it's a car.

It is always amazing what sticks in people's minds for passing on weeks or months later. This is from another Australian letter. The writer, a part-time journalist, meets the leader of the opposition at a state legislature.

> POLITICIAN: *I have a son called Justin.*
> *Me: You're joking! We almost called our eldest Justin.*
> *Politician: What did you call your son?*
> *Me: Jason.*
> *Politician: You're joking, we almost called ours Jason.*

Thanks to the miracle of airmail, that astounding coincidence could be across the world in a matter of days.

Some people find the process of preparing for Christmas a topic of endless interest:

> HAVE *you managed to complete your Christmas shopping yet? I think I have managed to do most of mine and have nearly done the wrapping. I am waiting now to put letters into parcels. I have a few more cards to write.*

From New Zealand:

> AT LAST *I have found time to get around to typing my Xmas newsletter — you will probably wonder at the early date, and no doubt you will receive this well before Christmas. However, if I get it in the post by 31st October, I will only have to pay $1 instead of*

$1.50. As I have 12 overseas letters, this will save $6.

Sometimes interesting nuggets can be found even after the holiday season. This is the gripping start of one lengthy letter:

AFTER *the Christmas and New Year celebrations, it was time for the more humdrum tasks — the first of which was getting the car through the MOT.*

Or this:

THE *paper was part of some recent work I've been doing on pre-Socratic philosophy. In due course some of the results of it will emerge in the form of a little book on the subject, hopefully in time for Christmas presents next year.*

It is extraordinary how some people imagine the rest of us will be intrigued by the day-to-day detail of their lives, even when those lives are as workaday as anyone else's. Take this family in Derbyshire:

HERE'S *a typical day:*
7.00 a.m. — the house stirs — Jack always up first, Jim or Deirdre battling to see who gets up last!
8.00 a.m. — Cello and violin practice
8.00 a.m. — (or sometime soon after) Jim trots down to college
8.10 a.m. — Emma takes the bus to school
8.35 a.m. — Jack and Charles escorted by foot to school

9.00 a.m. – Deirdre starts work

This goes on, hour by hour, until:

5.30 Jim is meant to arrive home, and the fun of evening activities begins.

This turns out to mean homework, followed by reading, baths and bedtime. They have even provided a seven-segment pie chart in full colour, indicating all the activities they get up to throughout the week:

Thur: boys have swimming lessons, Charles has Beavers, Deirdre has Housegroup...

The result is that it is possible for us to know, with a fair degree of accuracy, exactly what every member of the family is doing at any given moment in the year. Sadly, the recipient who sent the letter on indicated that he hadn't seen the parents for ten years and had never met – or shown any interest in – their children.

But some people love to describe their quotidian round:

I HAVE *reorganized my study and bought a new saddlechair (an osteopathic wonder, like a saddle on a pole) which is higher than my old office chair.*

Later the same writer reveals that 'Teazel has died' without revealing who or what Teazel might have been.

Many continue to pick over their lives like chimps plucking lice from each other's backs:

> JANET *continues her peripatetic experience of the criminal justice system. She has joined the probation staff, and also works part time (Thursdays, Fridays and every other Wednesday unless the week has a Bank Holiday in it, in which case for every other such week, she does a Monday instead of a Thursday, except in July and August).*

An air of desperation clings to some letters, as the writers search for something – anything – to pass along. These moments are from one family in Hampshire:

> TELEVISION *viewing has included many episodes of Friends… Table tennis has been less good, with even younger opponents beating me… Premium bond prizes totalled £350 in the year, the best so far, but lacking a Big One. Lottery results were similar, £215… A fiftieth anniversary was Roger Bannister's first under-4 minute mile in Oxford on 6 May 1954. I was so nearly there, but the rain cancelled my tennis match and I never left Cambridge…*

> IN TEDDINGTON, *a lot more ladies' hairdressers have opened this year, and a Thai restaurant.*

Or:

> THE LAST *four rams were sold four days before Jenny went into hospital. She hopes to have the second knee renewed in March.*

Some people have a gift for inflicting hundreds of words of detail, lulling the reader into a sense of false boredom, before dropping a nuclear device. This is all from one letter:

THE *following day we had a family gathering which most of you know was a complete disaster...*

No explanation is offered for those of us who don't know. Then:

February saw Harry's 2nd birthday which was spent at home with thirteen toddlers (!!!!!) We had a fantastic, albeit hectic time, until one of my friends decided to let her waters break right in the middle of our conservatory!!! I went to see a clairvoyant with Mum and Dad and was contacted by my Dad's Dad who I have never met. I took Harry to see Bill & Ben and Andy Pandy live in concert... at the same clairvoyant I was contacted by my Dad's Dad and my best friend's Mum's Mum... we had our garage converted into a study to add value to the house, and Robert and I decided to separate.

This news comes two thirds of the way through a letter that is otherwise unexceptional in its stress on humdrum detail.

One family brings what they clearly feel are intriguing tidings about their daughter settling into a new flat.

SHE *now has her own washing machine. No longer, therefore, does she need to bring washing home each weekend. She has her own kettle and tea pot, and all sorts of things... during one of her many shopping expeditions she bought a whole lot of plants, herbs and little bushes, and also food, watering cans, and secateurs… I now go to London on an almost monthly basis. The vegetables suffer a bit.*

Or take this newsflash from another letter:

ON THE *home front, Jonathan had his first rugby club dinner. An interesting array of drinks were served including beer with vodka and spring onions. Jonny made it home relatively unscathed, in contrast to one of his friends, who regurgitated in the back of his father's BMW and was grounded until the smell had gone.*

Hobbies can be a source of deep and abiding boredom:

THROUGH *much of this year I have been working hard on cataloguing our local railway museum's exhibits and books. Almost all of them are now listed and I've put together folders of the information, but I am woefully short of knowledge of some of the items. I've learned a lot and, for example, now know what a bolster plate is, and what the numbers mean on signal lever plates.*

This man, who comes from the West Midlands but has emigrated to Australia, is apparently obsessed by bikes. However, he has managed to put his pastime to good use. In 1996 he wrote to his friends (and I have altered the location of his work):

I TRIED *to capitalize on my five years as a 'cycling officer' by*

submitting a paper to the prestigious VeloAustralis conference in Western Australia. Not only was my paper accepted but I won the conference's Prize Paper competition! This led to two big coups in the following year: being nominated to the Trans-Tasman bicycle planning inter-governmental body, and in the last two months being awarded a study grant to prepare a 'foundation document' for a possible Tasmanian Cycling Strategy.

One year later, things have raced ahead:

The Tasmanian Cycling Strategy Foundation Project, with a target end date of September this year, has grown like Topsy. A change of government had a teeny bit to do with that. Some very important people have been beating paths to my door. Mine is the only project grappling with an area where policy-makers know full well there is a gap in thinking, with political imperatives for it to be filled… all this 'fame' has got us as a family gearing up to what might become of it.

The excitement and the stress are almost too much. Next year:

In October, I collapsed in a heap after having finished the final report of my year-long Tasmanian Cycling Strategy Foundation Project. A fancy title, basically just me beavering away on occasional days off work, but over the years I have gained some praise. It was six months before I recovered from my burn-out.

Worse is to come, for it turns out that the project wasn't finished after all. One year later:

> As I write this I am heaving a vast sigh of relief from at last
> finishing the final touches to my Tasmanian Cycling Strategy
> Foundation Project. The last completion tasks have been hanging
> over me.

But why, since it was clearly such a vast undertaking, did he ever start?

> I took on this project because of lies I had discovered in 1999
> being spread about me behind my back, and I needed to do
> something off my own initiative to clear my name. The downside of
> a project this narrow is that some now see me as having a fetish
> about bikes.

We are not told what these lies might be. 'He is a very interesting person,' perhaps.

One curiosity we have already noted is the way that the writers of these letters will often include long lists of names without any indication who the people might be – indeed only those recipients with an intimate knowledge of the senders' lives might be expected to recognize the names, and they would probably be familiar with most of the information already.

Take this family in London:

WE STARTED *the year with an early break, joining Marty, Justine and Adrian in Munich, before going to Austria for a week's skiing... we spent the weekend in Wales with our friend Hattie... another trip to Wales, this time to see Diane... we didn't have a Big Holiday, that's next year, and you will have to wait to read about it.*

I'm sure we can possess our souls in patience for another twelve months. They continue:

But we did go to the Isle of Wight to see Angela and Joe, and had a few weekends in Wiltshire and St Ives, managing to see Tess on our first trip to Cornwall where it obligingly stayed misty for two days... David, Erica, Sinead and Paddy are on the point of moving house... Kirsty and Lance are expecting another baby, so here's hoping for a new brother or sister for Bronwen and Kevin by Christmas. Christine and Hughie are both doing well, Hughie having made fantastic progress with his epilepsy over the year.

The recipients point out that 'not one of the people mentioned is known to us'.

Or take this family in East Anglia:

IN JANUARY I decided that I would go up to Yorkshire to Ralph. I had also not met Bill's mother, Jerry's partner, Dottie... in March I stayed with my old friend Jane Barrett... and in May it was back to the West Country again, visiting Chrissie and meeting her

husband Derek in their lovely old cottage, and on to Tom and
Bridget, whose garden was, as usual, lovely, and whose orchard pond
Arthur spent a happy morning helping to clear of weed. Then back
to James and Polly in Somerset… June saw us off on our annual
holiday with Charlotte and the pony. Leyla was there too… in
August it was the family holiday near Oban, Tom and Bridget were
there too… we started off in Kerry where Veronica took a really
hairy boat ride… I have been down to Sussex where Jessica's Pete
broke a leg playing football… Jolyon has fallen in love with
Barcelona… his extended family came over from Oxford and we
enjoyed Luke and Jen's company. Tilly is now a fully qualified
chiropodist, Ivor is head of science at his school, where Holly is
making good progress with her GCSEs. Pamela is now teaching full
time, Andy is picture-framing again, Barry is doing great things
with the Scouts, and Alec and Bronwen are continuing to police
south Norfolk. They are governors of their school, where Freda and
Geoff and Tim will also join them next year… Matthew is now a
chaplain at his college, and Alfie and Terence visited us for the first
time. At Christmas we were 18 for lunch. Do drop in if you are
passing.

Only eighteen for lunch? What happened to everyone else?

But these people are mere amateurs compared to some. The
heroes and heroines of descriptive detail don't just write; they
download. In some cases you suspect that it must have taken them

almost as long to write up the events in their lives as it did to experience them. Take this letter from Wales, which is approximately 9,000 words long. Nothing is too trivial to escape the writer's attention – the weather, a bus journey, a dispute over planning permission, an over-priced haircut – all are thrown into the hopper.

> THOSE *who knew my late brother, Eric, who died in 1998, may be interested to know that his last remaining asset, the spare head for his flute, which had lain in a wind instrument shop near Waterloo for about four years, was finally sold recently for £410. In January 2002 Francis visited the museum of musical instruments in Oxford to make sure his flute, which he had donated, was actually there. It was an unusual instrument, having been adapted by him, whereby his thumb took the place of his index finger, which he lost in an industrial accident.*

The writer, Francis, thoughtfully wishes to transfer his shares in the family pump-making business in order to benefit its employees. But the path to virtue is strewn with the boulders of difficulty:

> *To my annoyance, the company's auditors, whose assistance is needed, have upped sticks from their very convenient offices in the centre of town midway between the station and the factory and have gone off into the wilderness on the city's outskirts, very convenient*

*if you are heading for Birmingham, but otherwise remote and
difficult to find.*

He goes on:

*Talking of politics, Francis was persuaded to address a Fabian
Society 'Field Day' here on the subject of 'How to manage a Welsh
market town'. This is the first time he has been asked to do
anything in all his years of membership. Apparently it was
considered sufficiently amusing and thought-provoking, and he was
almost asked to repeat it at their Welsh annual conference.*

There is a world of lost fulfilment in that 'almost'. Nevertheless
life goes on in its fascinating way.

*Our vacuum cleaner gave up this year. However, by visiting the staff
shop at the Hoover factory in Merthyr we got a replacement for
about half the normal retail price, though getting it home on the
bus was a bit of a burden. It works well.*

Topics of even greater moment must be contemplated too. For
example, planning permission.

*All this is being overshadowed by no less than three recent schemes
across the river to create (a) an extended supermarket, (b) a
Homebase, plus car show rooms, warehouses etc., and (c) worst of
all, to develop the site of one of our few factories, now transferring
elsewhere, as a Retail Park. This last would contravene present*

planning policy on out of town developments and could have very
serious knock-on effects on the town's existing shops. Watch our next
Xmas newsletter for the outcome!

This is the point at which Christmas in a year's time seems almost
unbearable. Will we have to remember what the row was about?
Will he remind us which particular monstrosity was (a), (b) or (c)?
Are we obliged to care? In a sense it's possible to envy people who
are so easily engaged even by the drearier details of their sur-
roundings. For them life can never be dull.

And now we have the County's Unitary Development Plan
Amendments, and the South Wales Transport Board's Regional
Public Transport Strategy both requiring urgent attention before
meetings later this week!

My favourite comes from a couple who contributed heavily to the
companion volume, *The Cat that Could Open the Fridge*. This is their
twenty-fifth newsletter. It is twelve pages of small type, illustrated
by photos, some interesting ('Gators basking in the sun') others
less so, ('Mike making a phone call from the A46 during a traffic
jam.') The writer specializes in long, minute-by-minute accounts
of the holidays he and his wife enjoy.

TENERIFE. *Someone had the bright idea of getting an early*
morning flight, which meant getting up at 2.45, leaving at 4,
checking in at 5, and flying at 7. This meant, of course, going to

*bed at 8.30 the night before. At 2.45 the radio was doing features
I often catch just before I go to bed.*

They arrive, and as you might expect, their experiences getting a
cab provide plenty of material for the newsletter!

*We had pre-booked a taxi and were expecting to see a board
with our name on it in among all the other boards, and instead it
had the taxi firm's name on and the driver was in baggage
reclaim. We eventually got the attention of the controller, who took
our money for the outward and return trips and did the
paperwork, 48 euros for the return trip in a minibus with a 'Mar y
Sol' sticker.*

Their next trip is to a gîte in France, where a dilatory landlady
provides more chuckles:

*We got to Le Tasceau by 1.30, so stopped for a sandwich and a
final check of the way to the gîte, being two hours early. We
weren't expected till 4 or 4.30, so when we turned up at 2.30 the
landlady hadn't finished drying the sheets, but that was the only
thing that wasn't ready, so she let us install ourselves and promised
to bring the sheets and make the bed later. 4 o'clock passed, and
then 5, and still no sheets. At 6 I went to find her and she
promised them straight away. At 8.30 she turned up and we were
finally fixed up!*

There's no lack of fun while they're in the gîte, either.

The previous tenants had found the Nostalgie *station on the radio and we find it quite pleasant, if a little repetitive. Many of the hits were rendered into French by the stars of the day — we've just been treated to Del Shannon's 'Runaway' rendered as 'Loin de Moi', but I don't know by whom.*

Each day brings new excitements. He leaves his filler cap behind at a petrol station, but is able to buy a new one. They have a meal out, next door to an office party, whose departure makes the restaurant feel empty. It rains, but fortunately they had brought their macs with them. And before you know it, they're off to Florida to try out a timeshare. There's plenty of material in the differences between British and American cars.

Unable to find a handbrake I had to use the footbrake until I read in the handbook about a parking brake which is set using an auxiliary pedal and released using a manual catch…

They go to visit a lighthouse.

I climbed the 203 steps to the top but forgot to take a camera, so do not have any pictures of the views. As it was designated a museum there was no food or drink allowed on site. Drinking fountains were provided, but not cups. I could manage all right cupping my hands, but Dolly tried this and got soaked. Then she remembered her

origami skills from Girl Guides, fashioned a cup from a piece of
paper and was able to slake her thirst without further mishap.
While I was climbing the tower she sat and chatted to a visiting
Sunday school teacher who was looking out for things to tell her
class, so this was something she could use.

Yes, they discovered someone as fascinated by minuscule detail as they are! You wonder if the Sunday school teacher found the missing handbrake useful. ('You know, in this modern world it's not always easy to say "Whoa, stop!" But Jesus has provided a parking brake for you. You just need to find out where it is...')

The colourful kaleidoscope of these people's lives continues to be shaken up. The electric garage door is faulty, so they report it to the management. The weather is almost warm enough for a swim, but not quite, so they get out the jigsaw and start work on the edge pieces, though not until they have rearranged the lights in the apartment to make it easier to see. He cooks steak with courgettes ('known here as zucchini') and Dolly compliments him on his cooking. Finally they fly home, remembering to pack scissors, knives etc in their hold baggage. At one point he gives away his secret – he is looking for a special computer keyboard 'so I won't have to carry this laptop around', implying that he makes notes as he goes along, and need not let the tiniest detail be forgotten.

When they land, there is one final despairing cry:

Parking for two weeks at Gatwick costs us £288, which is more than double what we had been given to expect.

The holidays are covered in 4,300 words. And they have bought a timeshare, so we can all look forward to plenty more next year.

The Melancholy Mawkishness of Misery

IT IS A MYTH that all the writers of round robin letters want to boast. Many of them want to moan. Some of them moan at quite remarkable length. For some, no newsletter is complete without a detailed description of every single thing that has gone wrong with their lives. Tragically this does not always elicit the response they are presumably hoping for – pity, sympathy and regret. Just as often they get shouts of heartless glee.

> I KNOW *I shouldn't, but this litany of horrors just had me folded up with laughter. I hardly know these people anyway, so why do they think they can inflict all their miseries on us?*

That, I imagine, is the point. If these were people we knew well we would already be aware of all the woes that have afflicted them. Since in most cases they are people we know only distantly, or perhaps haven't met for decades, the cumulative effect is, sadly, quite hilarious.

Take this particular couple, who managed nine trips in the course of the year, almost all of them marked by moments of major medical distress:

WE HAD our usual seven weeks in Tenerife at the beginning of the year, but this was marked by a change in my medication which resulted in my feeling sick a lot of the time, so we didn't eat out much or dance much, in fact I lost well over half a stone. We spent a week in Kent in April with another change in my medication but the upset stomach continued which made me think I had something wrong with me. Eventually I left off all medication, mainly anti-inflammatory tablets and massage cream, and reverted to the original blood pressure tablets and things improved… in June I started with Plantar Fasciitis (pain in the heel) which stopped my gallop but not my dancing… in July we had booked to go to a health farm, but this had to be cancelled. Stanley developed a very swollen leg and foot, and after two weeks of antibiotics was still having to crawl on all fours to get about the house so the doctor sent him to hospital for a week. This allowed him to take the antibiotics directly into the vein via a drip. We are both on the move again now… we are all well now, but Stanley and I are not as supple as we were and getting up from a crouching position is quite an art in itself.

Or take this unfortunate chap:

HEALTH-WISE I have not been at my best since mid-September. While in Belgium, I was taking lots of medication on a regular basis, one for gout prevention, one for mild diabetes, one for high blood pressure and cardio-aspirin. All these four reacted together

and created a condition called auto-immune hepatitis, where the
body forms antibodies which attack the liver. This causes jaundice
and persistent itching. I spent two weeks in hospital in mid-
October, and have been recovering ever since. It is strictly no alcohol
for me! As a result of these strictures, I have lost almost four stone in
weight. This is weight I needed to lose, but I would not have chosen
this way to do it. I trust that you are in better health than me.

Some people, however, keep their spirits up and manage to find
consolations even in the midst of the medical mayhem:

OUR holiday in Granada completely lived up to all our
expectations — the only cloud being Sally's limited mobility because
of her replacement left shoulder, necessitated by a bad fall in April.
She was absolutely determined that the holiday should go ahead,
despite her pain and difficulties with only one functioning arm,
and was able to cope admirably... Life proceeded normally until
the August bank holiday when Dottie and Charles were doing their
periodic round-up of UK friends and family. We were meeting
Charles's two nice sons, Eric stepped into the road to view a
monument on the other side, only to be knocked down by a racing
cyclist (little pointy helmet, head down, no thought of slowing
down at the junction!) Poor Eric ended up later in the day when his
left arm was decidedly painful in the A&E department in the
county hospital. He was X-rayed and pronounced to have a Colles's
Fracture. He was then delivered to the Plasterer-in-Chief and we

finally arrived back home at about 8 p.m. after a two-hour session at the hospital... Charles's autobiography, a fascinating account of the professionalism of the ambulance service, was published in November – From Blue Lights to Brazil Nuts *– a very good read!*

Consolation can be found in many unexpected places, such as other people's sickness:

WE *hope this letter finds you well and content with life. This has been a 'different' year for us, with ups and downs. On 1 March 2004 at 2.45, Simon and Peta were informed that Simon had prostate cancer. After a few months and some soul searching we chose the surgery option, and an operation was performed in June. Simon's recovery has been excellent and a recent test was not able to detect prostate cells in the blood... It was a shock because there were no symptoms. We can only ponder over situations like that of Simon's old friend Douglas Marsland, rendered quadriplegic by a car accident in January.*

Some illnesses are less dramatic, but still earn their place in the annual round-up:

PADDY *and Janet are keeping well. Paddy has been diagnosed with Parkinson's Disease. At the moment he is wearing Darren's sandals, as he has had to have both his big toenails off, having had ingrowing toenails.*

Others affect a certain stiff upper-lipped insouciance:

> BY FAR the best thing, if not the pleasantest thing I did this year,
> was to part company with my gall bladder.

Or this, from Australia:

> BARRY has recently recovered from kidney stones which caused him
> twelve days of agony and three visits to hospital to have pain-
> killing injections. He finally passed the stones and lots of gravel,
> and is back to his old self again. Thank goodness he is, as we have
> had some terrible storms with giant branches coming down, electric
> fences for the horses being blown down, the swimming pool full of
> debris. We thought at one point the horses would float out of the
> paddock, it was so flooded.

Some people seem to have no luck at all:

> MARIAN still struggles with her medical complications from Lupus
> and Scleroderma. The jaw infection has been modified but not
> eliminated yet. She is scheduled for an oesophagus stretch on
> December 15. She is also trying to get her ulcers under control
> before then, to avoid complications. However, she is very happy and
> enjoys her quality of life as much as is humanly possible. She is
> finally slowing down her real estate practice.

Hardly surprising. You wonder how she could possibly have
coped.

You also have to wonder about some people's priorities. Take this letter from the south-east and its list of curiously mixed incidents:

> IF THE LAST *you heard from us was last Christmas, you'll be pleased to know that we did eventually get our new central heating boiler installed just before Christmas, but that was just the beginning of the fun!*

You idly ponder why the writers imagine that people they haven't felt the need to contact through an entire year would have the faintest interest in their new boiler. Still, on they plough:

> *Late on Christmas eve, Julie managed to snap the bathroom door key as she tried to unlock it. Fortunately it was the ground-floor bathroom, so Felix was able to rescue her through the window, but that still left the problem of the locked bathroom. Finally, by around 2 a.m. on Christmas morning, Christian managed to fashion a key out of a piece of sheet brass that he happened to have around.*

Again, you wonder why the recipients should be fascinated by an event that took place fully a year before.

> *No sooner had our first guests departed than we got a call to say that my (Joanne's) Mum had fallen out of bed in her new care home, had fractured a femur, and was in hospital… Christmas / New Year was also punctuated by a dead phone line, which led to a*

telephone engineer crawling around our loft on New Year's Day, and a dead freezer which Christian managed to fix by thawing an ice blockage with a hair dryer. Nearly all our visitors were full of coughs and bugs, so I had to cancel a restaurant booking for nine, and set to produce yet more food from scratch.

In February a routine scan showed that I had breast cancer...

Keeping cheerful after breast cancer is something our round-robinners do well.

IN APRIL *Mum, 80 next March, was found to have a small breast cancer lump, which was discovered during her annual visit to hospital. This was successfully removed in June, followed by a course of radiotherapy, and she is now OK, the only apparent after-effect being the craving for a new kitchen.*

Indeed, when illness strikes perkiness is always at a premium:

AILMENTS *this year — nothing spectacular but a new phenomenon is Patrick's left knee. In the silence of the dawn his patella can be heard clicking and cracking like a rifle bolt being engaged as he makes his routine visit to the khazi at 7 a.m. Dr Shaw gave his considered opinion: 'It's buggered — what do you expect at your age?'... Mother-in-law had surgery on her nose and she now has a prosthesis which is remarkably like her old nose, down to the blemishes and capillaries.*

This newsletter is from the Midlands:

> OUR DEAR friend Wendy, whose Scottish wedding was reported
> here last year, has a spinal condition caused by a car accident a few
> years ago. She sought relief by buying a huge inflated ball to sit on.
> Recommended by physiotherapists, these are supposedly burst-proof.
> Not so! One evening, Wendy was sitting on hers watching the telly
> when it went bang, and dropped her instantly two feet onto her
> coccyx, giving her concussion and temporary paralysis and putting
> her in great pain. It had medicos seriously worried for a while.
> Fortunately she seems to be recovering now. Needless to say, a law
> suit is in the offing. Meanwhile if you have balls like these, don't sit
> on them.

We will bear that in mind. Good humour can leaven the grief.
This is from a woman in Surrey:

> MY fibromyalgia has settled into a vague pattern, in that most of
> the time I can forget that I have it (hooray!). However, there are
> months when the pain, fatigue and feelings of hopelessness engulf
> me, and I just have to accept a week or so of feeling disgusting until
> it lifts. Then there's the dystonia. This takes many forms, and the
> one I have is spasmodic torticollis (which my computer's spell check
> keeps trying to change to 'portcullis'!), which causes
> uncontrollable, unpredictable shaking of the head. At present it is
> a very mild tremor, but it is a progressive condition and the

neurologist cannot say how bad it will get. Some unfortunate
sufferers find themselves 'stuck' with their head at an unfortunate
angle, and require botox injections (no comments about face lifts,
please!)... another diagnosis this year was of multiple allergies,
after I had a severe attack in the night that left me unable to
swallow, close my mouth, or look anything like a human being. The
allergist found that I am allergic to nuts, wheat, citrus, raw onions
and tomatoes... my back is better than it has been for years...

Thank goodness there is some good news. Again, the letter would
be dreadful if you knew the person well; as it is you have a vague
feeling that there is nothing you can do, and a mild resentment
that so much unhappiness should be dumped on your doorstep in
the festive season.

For some people, life is a deep sea swell of misery alternating
with delight. These people's nephew pops over from Canada and
they have a marvellous time. Then:

IN MAY *Dennis got chicken pox and very kindly passed it on to me.*
We were both very ill and I am still bearing the scars. One at least
looks like being permanent. No, I did not pick it — the scab just
came off in the night.

Whoa, as the Americans say, too much sharing!
Next they have a really great holiday in Kenya. But another
wave threatens to capsize their lives:

I returned to work refreshed and raring to go, only to be told that my job was at risk of redundancy. I left on December 3rd. I am somewhat upset, to say the least.

But the year ends with a successful church craft 'fayre', so it has not been a complete write-off.

It may be my imagination, but there seems to be quite a high mortality rate among relatives of the people who send Christmas newsletters. But they never let the Grim Reaper spoil their lives:

IN JUNE we had a nice holiday in North Wales, with all three of the boys with us for the first weekend, in which we scattered my mother's ashes in one of her favourite beauty spots. It was a very moving and positive experience — AND a good holiday! I am attaching a poem which was read during the ceremony. And we had a nice meal in a pub, afterwards.

In round robin-land, every cloud has a silver lining.

WE are very grateful that my father did not suffer much pain. His electronic organ was donated to the residential home, and we understand that the local organ society has organized a roster to play to the residents.

SADLY, my Mum died of leukaemia shortly after Christmas. We miss her dreadfully. Trevor's poor Mum died the previous June after suffering a very long protracted period of Parkinson's disease, a

truly dreadful illness. They are both at peace now, but sadly missed.
Trevor's Dad, understandably, is finding it very difficult coping
with the loss and amongst other things he has had treatment for
depression. We try very hard to encourage him to get out and about,
but he seems very reluctant to leave home these days.

Well, enough of the gloomy news, now for the nail-biting stuff.
Ed is in his gap year, and martial arts still feature prominently in
his life...

UNFORTUNATELY, *Uncle James has been quite poorly for the last*
six months — we are due to have some results later this week, but
things are not looking good at the moment and he is being very brave.

We enjoyed a lovely holiday in the Vendée in August, which we
would thoroughly recommend...

If life gives our writers lemons, they get briskly to work, making
lemonade:

THIS *year of course started in the most traumatic way, with Mum's*
funeral in Devon. Although it was a wonderful occasion, especially
to see so many of the family present at the church, it brought to a
close the end of an era, with Mum at 91 being the last of her
generation on the family tree. During the whole of the year,
following our fantastic trip with her to Oz, it was so sad to watch
her slowly leaving us in her mind, when she had been such an
active, caring and bubbly person.

Well, to make up for all that sadness, Janet and I have just booked a 12-day Canary Island cruise, starting from Italy...

THIS *autumn was the truly sad part of the year. Jacob's Mum, Margaret, has had Parkinson's for some time and had become increasingly immobile as a consequence. She had only been in her nursing home for a month when she had a stroke, and died that same evening. So sad, but as Jacob said, we don't have to worry about her any more... The church was packed to hear Jacob give a very moving address. Tea and cakes after at the tea-room next to her house, and a pub meal in the evening for all those who stayed. We'd had a similar meal in the same pub after Jacob's Dad died, and Margaret enjoyed it so much she asked if we could do it annually.*

LET'S *get it over with — at the beginning of June our beloved Shaun, that gentle giant of a fellow, took his own life. He had been suffering from stress and depression for a short time caused, probably as always, by overwork... it has been very hard on both of us as the grief caused the family to pull in opposite directions and we have been so very grateful for all the support we have received from the rest of the family and our friends.*

Sad bit of the letter over, let's get onto the happier times. For Nick's birthday treat I decided that we would have a day trip to Venice and have a romantic trip on a gondola...

Here is another letter, in which the most appalling misfortunes do nothing to reduce the relentless breeziness:

> MY STEPFATHER, Gordon, had a major stroke and was admitted to hospital a few hours later as an emergency. They thought he was a 'goner', but has made virtually a 100 per cent recovery and is now playing golf and bridge regularly… the really sad outcome of the stroke was that my Mum, Gwyneth, had to go into a home as she had advancing Alzheimer's and was being looked after by my stepfather. The home and Mum didn't work out so, after four nights, she had to be admitted to the Memorial Hospital. After she was chucked out of there in August, we managed to get her into another home, but she died peacefully there four weeks later… my sister was having tests and then had to go into hospital for a major op. Fortunately it turned out to be a massive ovarian cyst and not cancer (some good news, at last!).
>
> Things were just beginning to settle down again and we were all making plans for a reduced family Christmas when my brother-in-law Alan had a major stroke last week. He is likely to be totally paralyzed down his left side (luckily he is right-handed). The stroke has not affected his comprehension or speech, but there seems to be little sign at this stage of any physical recovery… Jim's round of health checks ended up with him being diagnosed with allergy / exercise-induced asthma, a hiatus hernia and an 'irritable' digestive system. He reckons he's had every orifice violated this year at least once.

They try to forget all this misery by going on holiday to France, where it rains. Their house is still falling down. But that's not all:

Cats are still with us but living on the edge – there is a constant territory battle going on with a black 'puma' that's moved into the areas, and our two 'wussy pussies' are losing. It even stands up to us, and is extremely vicious, despite several soakings with my new water gun!!! War is declared.

Yes, nothing – not death, disease or disappointment – can keep down our writers' quirkiness quotient.

It HAS been a mixed year to say the least. Our Aunty died. She was my Mum's surviving sister. It was a real strain for Doris to attend the funeral but she did it. Then, our cousin's wife died after a brave fight against her illness. I went on my own to her funeral, as Doris did not feel up to it. My friend, whom I have known since I was twenty, is now in a nursing home. Another friend was very ill, so I managed to few day trips to north London to visit them. Sadly, the first friend is no longer with us.

Whether or not it was caused by stress, Doris developed a bowel problem. She underwent tests which revealed there was nothing malignant. You can imagine what a relief that was! Currently I have two friends who are undergoing 'chemo' treatment.

Jasper, my dog, had problems. Lots of visits to the vet solved nothing so he was referred to the Animal Trust hospital, where tests

*revealed that he has an inflammatory bowel condition. The cat is
fine.*

Phew! But the relief is transient:

*Lesley has been suffering from a viral infection of the ear. It is
stable, so we hope it will remain so. My neighbour across the road
broke the top of her leg about thirteen weeks ago. She was well on
the way to recovery when a pin came adrift so she had to go back
into hospital for a hip replacement.*

*We spent last Christmas at the local hospital where Doris's
husband was. We enjoyed the time, which may sound odd, but
Harold had two much better days. Christmas Day he ate a little
'real' food – Christmas dinner and fresh salmon for tea. During the
afternoon we took him, in a chair, for a walk round the hospital
corridors where we could look at all the paintings, before sitting in
the canteen area to have a carton of juice. Harold fancied a piece of
chocolate, but that made him choke so he couldn't eat much.*

*On the ward, while he slept, we played Hangman, Noughts and
Crosses, and I Spy. It is amazing how the time flew. Sadly Harold
died at the end of January. Those two days at Christmas, therefore,
seem extra special.*

Does all this death make us downhearted? No! She continues:

*I provide plenty of amusement with my forgetfulness. The one which
takes the biscuit happened recently. I could not find my watch. I*

thought back to when I last remembered taking it off. When I washed up after the Mothers' Union meeting? Telephone call to Jacqui — out — so I left a message. Telephone the rector — out — so left a message. Then I decided to get on with household tasks, rolled up my sleeve and THERE was the watch, up my arm! Oh well!! Two more telephone calls…

Take this couple who go to stay at a favourite hotel in Wales.

UNFORTUNATELY *the lady who owns the hotel is fighting liver cancer. It is the one occasion I forgot to leave our telephone number at home, and our mobiles were off. Donald, who many of you knew, who lived with us for many years, and was like a grandfather to the children, died suddenly the day after we arrived. Pat could not make contact, but she was very good and did all the administrative work. We did continue our holiday, played golf on two courses, and visited Anglesey. When we returned there was a letter from the Bishop of _____ , whose wife owns the cottage we rent in Scotland, to say that her mother had died… to continue the death saga, Mark's cousin's wife told us at Don's funeral that her mother had died the previous day, so we had another funeral the following week… Dennis's girlfriend, poor girl, has just had a polyp removed which extended from the nose to the brain. It was a seven-hour operation… she is unable to eat solids… we all look forward to a happy and prosperous New Year and wish everyone good health and peace.*

Letters in the form of chronological diaries can create some alarming juxtapositions. This family from the south-east begins with the glad news about their little girl appearing as 'an angel (!) in her nursery school nativity play. She insists that she was a "Mangel"!' This news comes just before tidings of mother-in-law's final illness, which prevents her from attending the family Christmas party, and brings about her death four days later. Then the wife's father, Arthur, has a stroke:

> HE HAD *to go back regularly for blood transfusions. The doctors involved began to hint that something much more serious than his stroke was involved... Linda and Isobel went shopping on Saturday... towards the end of May we left for Zurich on a Saga holiday in Switzerland — a rail tour. Arthur had more blood transfusions.*
>
> *June: We returned to England after having had a wonderful time in Switzerland... we stayed in Lugano for four days in a large hotel next door to the railway station, with the main Switzerland to Italy line running via a level crossing across the hotel drive. Heaven for Alasdair, who sat up on the bedroom ledge one night watching freight trains at 4 a.m.*

They buy some pottery. Then they come home:

> *Sadly, Arthur's condition began to worsen rapidly, and we were made aware that he had a large laryngeal cancer. He died on the 13th.*

August: a relatively quiet month. We all went off together to Derbyshire for a mass clan holiday. Unfortunately this was spoiled by gastric flu breaking out.

September: another quiet month. Alasdair and Judi paid a visit to the Family History Centre, and unearthed what may be a minor skeleton in the family.

We are not told what this is, though given the family's recent history, a 'minor skeleton' might well be the bones of a dead child.

October: this month was marked by Frank's miraculous escape when the lorry he was driving caught fire on the A303. He was blown from the cab clutching only his mobile phone, and escaped without injury…

It is not only people whose misfortunes can cause havoc in others' lives. Take animals. These people live in Somerset and have turned their Christmas newsletter into a memorial, with pictures, for two of their pets, including Watson, their much-loved dog. As if it were a gravestone, the first page is emblazoned with the words 'WATSON. 10th April 1996 – 3rd July 2004' next to a large colour photo.

IN JANUARY a friend's dog jumped at Watson whilst he was tied up, causing the left leg to stick out sideways. It was thought to be his cruciate ligament again…

There follows a long saga of Watson's last months on this earth. Anti-inflammatories fail to work. He has an X-ray, and an orthopaedic surgeon diagnoses bone cancer. They take him to the Animal Health Trust where chemotherapy is recommended.

Watson's homoeopath then said...

There are homoeopathic vets? What do they prescribe? A one in ten million solution of Bonio?

... That we would anger the cancer and it would spread everywhere, rapidly. After much agonizing, we struggled through the snow and ice to the vet's for his op. Within a day Watson was already happy and hopping around...

They change his diet for cheaper food, which works wonders.

Never again will I use the so-called top of the range foods. He looked marvellous and his coat was even more glossy and silky than before... a few days later, the vet could not believe it, Watson should not have been able to walk. He had ruptured his cruciate, but was hopping around... then a few days later it fell apart... he was put to sleep in his favourite spot in the garden one sunny July morning.

The whole story occupies almost 600 words of the newsletter. But there is more to come. Their cat Denzil disappears and is found after four days in a neighbour's garage.

Luckily there was water, and he was fine. Five days after returning
from Sweden and two hours after finishing this letter, I found him
asleep on the sitting room chair. Except that he wasn't asleep. He
was dead.

Similarly, the end of the letter consists of a large, illustrated memorial to the late Denzil. The recipient says in his covering letter: 'I have never met the people in this circular, my wife hasn't seen them for over twenty years, yet each year we get bombarded with the minutiae of their lives. I have to confess that by the time I came to the news about the cat, I just burst out laughing.'

How heartless can you be? Actually very heartless if some of the covering notes are to be believed. And animals do seem to be unlucky. This is from people who live in the West Country:

ONE of our sheep is recovering from recurrent attacks of mange
(apparently rare in sheep but we specialize in unusual sheepish
ailments), another is laid to rest in our freezer after inexplicably
injuring itself. Both our pet rats died this year, and last week a
heron helped itself to all our fish, which were many and some quite
a good size… the rabbits (wild) are looking well on a varied diet
from my vegetable garden, in spite of elaborate barricades of old
fencing wire, fireguards etc. We have no ducks or chickens left as the
foxes keep eating them.

Family strife is sometimes a problem, especially as it can spoil the jaunty spirit of a Christmas letter.

> THE LAST *year has been the most difficult of our married life, so I am not going to bore you with the details, suffice it to say that a close family member died, Geoff lost the use of his right arm, and I had to spend eight weeks away from home.*

One way of handling it is to slip the bad news into the middle of the usual hectic excitement and achievement. This letter, from New England, is packed with news of swimming triumphs, sailing adventures, a vacation in the Adirondaks, an Easter egg hunt, Timmy's braces, which should be off by the end of 2006, a trip to Bermuda, a record tomato crop, and success at the local flower show. Then, apropos of nothing, and with no explanation offered:

> IN LATE *July, Preston moved out. Our divorce should be final some time next summer.*

Moments later, the kids are in summer camp, enjoying archery, canoeing and fishing.

But we all know that families can cause untold grief. Usually this is a topic newsletter writers steer well clear of, but here, from the Midlands, is a letter that explores the topic in a way that might even be comprehensible if you knew all the different individuals involved.

SADLY, *Mike's marriage to Pru (and consequently, his leaving his childhood home) seemed to be the catalyst for a rift in Robert's family that is still not completely healed. Briefly, the rift seems to have come about through a personality clash between Roger, Robert's middle brother, and Pru, and Bev's difficulty in letting Mike go. Theresa and Robert refused to take sides, but when Theresa tried to play 'peacemaker', she got caught in the 'crossfire'. The result for us was a time of great sadness, with Bev and Roger refusing to come to family occasions that Mike and Pru were invited to, including Kitty's birthday party in July and a lovely family party at Mike and Pru's new home the same month...*

Oh dear, but nothing a nice cup of tea and a chinwag won't sort out, I'm sure. But here is another example of the kind of hatred close relationships can inspire:

BEFORE *mid-morning Boxing Day the uneasy calm and equilibrium between my mother and I, managed so carefully the days before, slipped and toppled almost headlong into the pool, over some short sharp remarks of my mother's and my impatience over her endless nit-picking about ingredients in the food! Christmas just wouldn't have been the same — I would have missed those gut-churning emotions, timed to return me to the conscious search on the 'path of middle way' of Buddhist teaching, and to remember that 'this too will pass'.*

This comes from a letter from Florida:

> SORRY, *no Christmas letter this year. 2004 has been a very bad*
> *year, and the epistle would have been a tale of woe. We must keep in*
> *contact, so here is our wish to you: have a very Merry Christmas and*
> *a healthy and prosperous New Year.*

Underneath the writer has added by hand a morose footnote:

> *Luckily, no damage from the hurricane.*

Some letters are not actually miserable, but they do contain an underlying regret, a sense that the best life has to offer has passed the writer by.

> BIGGEST *news of all is that I have finished 'A Time of Quiet'! Yes,*
> *the first draft manuscript is printed — all 850 pages / 152,000*
> *words. Only problem is that my London agent has also gone quiet.*
> *Their web page shows they are in some sort of hiatus and there is no*
> *reply to e-mails or phone. I have a letter from them soliciting my*
> *MS and an e-mail acknowledging that I take my time, but now only*
> *silence.*

The awful thought occurs that the agents might have actually folded their business rather than read those 850 pages.

The next sorry tidings come from a couple who send their newsletter every year in the form of a nicely stapled and well-printed booklet. The pages are full of news and pictures of their many travels and their various political activities:

> AFTER *fiddling with it for nearly two years, Reg has finished his musical* ad hominem *attack on the alleged 'character' of George W. Bush. This opus 25 is called 'Bang!' which has much drumming in it. The music is very complicated, but it is trying to illustrate the workings of a quite capable but totally dysfunctional mind. He is working on something pleasanter now, for a chamber orchestra.*

They go to Spain for a holiday:

> *The Guggenheim is a great building, but most of the art inside is crap.*

Reg and Priscilla's socialist beliefs do not prevent them from being landlords. Indeed, they describe themselves as 'socialist land-lords'. This has led to problems, all of which are described in pitiless detail:

> *Warning — the hell of being a landlord. After everything going smoothly for several years, almost everything that could go wrong, did. Reg thought he had fixed a leak from Flat 4 into Flat 3, and redecorated Flat 3's bathroom. The tenants left in May on the day we went to France, so Reg had the prospect of more decorating on his return. When we did, he had not only to redecorate but the bathroom problem had recurred. He fixed it again and redecorated…*

You may feel that by now you know an adequate sufficiency about the flats and their problems. You would be mistaken.

... Meanwhile, three other tenants gave notice, leaving us with only two flats let... fortunately the new people wanted to decorate themselves...

By hanging Christmas tree ornaments on their body parts? Apparently not, but that's the kind of silly joke that creeps into your mind while reading this interminable saga...

... Although we paid for the materials. Phew! However, Reg did do their bathroom, not trusting tenants with this potential source of trouble... just as things seemed to settle down, the flat in Whitley Terrace flooded the flat below at appalling expense in repairs and compensation, as the tenant (not ours) was on holiday and his suits were covered in fungus when he got back. At the same time (and during Cilla's birthday party), the ceiling fell in on Flat 2's kitchen, filling the place with 144 years of under-floor dust, much to the rage of the tenant, who has since left. To add to her woes, Flat 3's bath tiles decided to leak into her bathroom and Reg had to take down part of that ceiling... to crown this, the loo in Flat 4 leaked and, while the new tenant took the initiative to fix it himself, the Flat 3 decoration was ruined for the third time. All this rather put the mockers on our trip to Greece... trying to be a good socialist landlord can be, err, trying.

There is more, much more of this. I suspect that somewhere in north London there are recipients of this newsletter who organize wine and nibbles parties, at which the whole story is read out loud to general hilarity.

Some people lead lives, not of quiet, but of noisy desperation. This is from Yorkshire:

> IT SEEMS *like only yesterday that I was writing to you last year. I must admit I will be glad to see the back of this year. In all honesty it has been the worst year of my life.*

Things start well when his second book is published, and he gives a lecture in Germany. Then his wife's aunt dies. In February his dad takes a sudden turn for the worse.

> *He had been making such good progress on the new treatment he was having, but then the cancer got a hold in his brain. The doctors were flabbergasted. It was only the second time they had seen this happen.*

Then an elderly relative of his wife dies, in the same ward as his father.

> *They were the worst things of the year, but fate had more things in store for us.*

He runs a business matching computer programs to services and products, but this was set back by all the illness. Then they meet the 'client from hell'.

By mid-September the relationship deteriorated to the point where we agreed to hand over all we had done and take a massive loss on all the work we had done, just to be rid of him. Within two days he broke the agreement, and demanded the return of the advance he had paid us. He made threatening phone calls (which interested the police) and set a debt collection agency on us... it has ended up that he is taking me to court... I have absolutely no confidence in the legal system.

We have made practically no progress on the home projects, nor has the kit car left the garage... we hope to see you soon but until then, a very happy Christmas and a superb 2005.

But these people live a life of bliss compared to the tortures undergone by some.

ANGELA'S *partner, Paul, was diagnosed a few months ago as ADD (attention deficit disorder). He is one of a growing number of adults being found to have this disorder. He has been put on medication to combat this. This sadly led to a mental condition to the extent that he held Angela and her mother hostage at the point of a gun for a day and a half. He allowed his sister to take Lottie out of the house after a time, but no one was allowed in, none of them out...*

Happily, it all ends peacefully, and the rest of the letter contains news of the remarkably gifted grandchildren.

This letter from the Midlands, which contains more misery per paragraph than any other this year, comes with a promise from the recipient that they have checked very carefully and discovered that it is not a spoof:

> HOPE *you are well, and looking forward to the festive season!*
>
> *Cyril faces having another heart operation in the next year, as although he has made a good recovery from the first, it was unsuccessful.*
>
> *Andrew _____ has been sentenced to life in prison without parole on three counts of 1st degree murder, he pleaded guilty without trial to avoid the death penalty. It is Cyril's wish to go to America to pick up some personal items, which the police are holding, but when we go will depend on Cyril's health.*

There is no mention of who Andrew _____ is, or who he is alleged to have murdered. Or why the writers should be picking up his personal effects. Still, life goes on, after a fashion.

> *We were all ready for our move to Devon in July when the sale fell through three days before completion. This was a devastating blow...*
>
> *Wishing you all a happy new year from us all!*

The Wickedness of Whimsy

SINCE PEOPLE these days are more self-conscious about round robin letters, they tend to worry that a straightforward recitation of the year's events will be received with mockery and resentment, and they are very often right. So they sometimes turn to whimsy, coyness, cloyingness, and worst of all, verse.

One of the most serious sins – and my sense is that the practice is spreading – is to write your letter as if from one of your pets. This may sound charming. But it does create a serious problem. You can remain 'in character' so to speak, and make the entire letter a dreary catalogue of events as seen through the eyes of the animal – mice killed, relationships with neighbouring pets, and so forth. This letter is from a British family living in Holland. They have four hens, each of which is allotted a section of the letter:

INTRODUCING: *Nuggets. First of all, I'd appreciate it if you refrained from making jokes about my name. It's lucky I'm not a Scot (McNuggets – get it?). I am a Welsum, a breed originating in Holland. I have exquisitely subtle and beautiful feathering and a gentle, calm temperament (a characteristic much needed in this coop, I can tell you!) Even though I am gentle, I am the lead hen –*

meaning I am top of the pecking order, and responsible for keeping
the others in line. I've not yet laid an egg. Productivity isn't really
my thing – strange considering my origins. When I do start laying,
the eggs will be a beautiful, rich dark brown colour, almost like
chocolate!

And so on, through her coop-mates ('my wattles will be plump,
red and elongated – truly divine' or 'I would rather be foraging
and exploring than writing, so I will sign off now with best
wishes.') The letter ends with a narcolepsy-inducing chart,
showing how many eggs each hen might be expected to produce
in the coming year.

An alternative to this toe-curling material is to kick off as if the
letter was being written by the pet, but then let them go into the
normal human accomplishments-and-holidays mode. This is
written as if by a cuddly toy.

SOME *of you will know me, Percy Penguin, from Julian's childhood.*
I am the small stuffed penguin who has influenced everything he
has done for the past thirty seven and a half years. So, what have I
done this year while avoiding the sticky clasp of a pink and yellow
Princess Fairy, My Little Pony-fixated two-year-old?

This turns out to be a reference to Julian's daughter. Soon poor
old Percy is writing in an uneasy mixture of furry penguin-speak
and normal adult discourse:

Jayne, who took over my job of minding Julian once he became a grown-up, has had a busy year at work. After seven years in Intel customer support, she has moved departments to become an expert in privacy and data protection. She now works with lawyers — a profession penguins have managed without.

The same difficulty applies to this American letter from Freckles, who turns out to be a dog.

ONE *night I was finding my favourite spot to poop by one of the trees along the fence by the Cathedral. When a man passed by, he pointed at me, and said: 'Yeah, that's what I want to be in my next life.'*

But soon Freckles drops these candid canine confessions and moves onto the rest of the family:

Sidney's article, about the utility of certain landfill materials for home insulation, appeared in Vol. I, No. 1, of the Beaufort Science Journal, *a magazine published through a program at our local teacher's college.*

This letter, from North-west England, is written entirely by the mole in the garden.

THE *highlight of the year was when they built the Mole Temple* [this turns out to be a shaded bench]. *It started out as 'an idea'. This was how she (the Mother human) put it when she was*

talking to him (the Father) one bright spring morning... perhaps I
should explain. Since my last newsletter to you twelve months ago,
my tunnels have increased tenfold.

News of the family's attempt to get rid of the mole is interleaved
with an account of the arrival of a pest control officer to kill the
rats. But soon we are back with intelligence about the family.

David, the one I call 'the Son', has deferred his second year of civil
engineering. He might look for a full-time job for a while... he
says that geo-technics is not his favourite area; he prefers urban
development...

The next letter, from a couple in the East Midlands, is written by
their cat, Lulu. This section comes after a lengthy description of
Lulu's life, which involves chasing mice and sleeping in the cold
frame.

MY JOB *as stroke therapist became especially significant this*
year... in the summer, Phil's mother became seriously ill, and she
died in the autumn. With all this I think I was appreciated more
than usual.

It does seem a little perverse to announce the death of your
mother-in-law through the fictional voice of your cat. The letter
goes on to become the usual uneasy mixture of winsome pet-talk
and family boasting:

Meanwhile my mistress went twice to lunch at Buckingham Palace.
The first lunch (with the Queen) was because it was discovered she
was a 'woman of achievement' (Wot?) along with Charlotte Church,
Margaret Thatcher, Julian Clary (?), the Superior of the Whitby
Sisters, and 497 others. The second time she had to say grace at a
garden party… even if she tries to play with the computer mouse, I
will walk on this keyboard. She has been warned — after five years
here, she needs, for once, to sit down long enough for me to sit on
her lap and purr. I am very good at purring.

The letter is, as you might expect, signed with a charming paw
print alongside the couple's e-mail addresses.

A recent and alarming development is getting your dead pets
to write your Christmas letter. This one, from a cat domiciled in
Essex, could bring some people out in hives:

ACTUALLY *the most affecting thing that happened in 2004, for*
the Hapgoods anyway, was that I died. I had been showing my age
(nearly eighteen) for a while, and one sunny autumn day I just
didn't wake up from my morning snooze on the patio. Jo cried a lot
(very gratifying) and in the afternoon she buried me in front of her
pottery pavilion (in a white cotton shroud, which made my
reception here in Heaven quite a respectful one — a lot of domestic
shorthairs turn up in cardboard boxes, which gets them off to a poor
start socially, especially with the Egyptians, who can be pretty
superior about their grave goods)… frankly it is a little dull up

here (now I know what she means about Geneva!) and I've not yet
had time for networking. Anyway, anyone who says that a dead cat
can't write just as well as a live one, is simply an ignorant
thanatist.

Yes, we can all agree that a dead cat writes precisely as well as a
live one. Before long the deceased feline is onto the topic of Iraq
and the competence of George W. Bush, winter fuel payments,
holidays and so forth.

There is a family in East Anglia, of distinctly mystic bent, who
for the second year running have cast their round robin in the form
of a message from their dead dog, Webster, who went 'to roam
the Elysian fields' more than a year before.

WELL, *I bet you weren't expecting to hear from me any more —*
dust to dust, ashes to ashes and all that — but even though my body
is now quite mummified in the sandy soil, I am not
incommunicado, and my spirit is still breezing around, along with
all the other departed Upper Farm souls.

The New Age beliefs and practices of Webster's former owners
make it sometimes hard to work out exactly what is happening,
especially as the dog presents the most humdrum activities, such
as getting the car repaired or visiting the supermarket, as if they
were scenes from a play. It's an extended storyboard rather than
a letter. Some sense of their lives emerges from what the late

Webster calls a 'Goddess list' and most of us would think of as things to do scribbled on the back of an envelope:

Order skip

Rat man

Write: Jude, Filly, Prim

Ring: King of Ireland [the name of a pub? Or possibly a bookmaker? We are not told], *Janet, Dominic*

Moles

Tackle cobwebs

Chicken corn

Bury duck

Financial Adviser — tel.

Qigong practice

Lysistratas

Clean larder

Drains

Nettles

Aga man

Family tree — start

Poetry — write

Pictures — paint

Publisher — contact

Pheasant — pluck

Arts For All — plan

Iraq — catch up on
Slurry — deal with
Knitting

This is no doubt supposed to convey a life crowded with daily activity, yet with time set aside for the artistic and the spiritual. The actual effect on the reader, however, is more likely to be 'why is she telling me this, is it going to be her laundry list next, and why is she doing it in the voice of a dog which is dead, and quite probably couldn't talk at all when it was still alive?'

But then some people's lives do seem to centre around their pets. This is from Wales:

A SADDER *event was the demise of Pele, Gabriel's iguana.*
Aficionados of the film ET *will remember the scenes where Eliot*
and ET exhibited parallel suffering, growing more and more
pathetic. Well, as Gabriel pined in his Manchester flat, Pele —
abandoned — pined away in Llandudno. Despite the valiant efforts
of the vet (who declared he had obviously had a good life and had
been well looked after) it was no good, and he now lies at peace
below the raspberry canes in the garden. In contrast, Nick's snakes
continue to flourish, growing ever larger and more vicious. Gwynn's
pond fish, who have probably not had a mention in these letters
before, have thrived for about three years, but yesterday he
discovered that only one was remaining from the original six, and
today he was horrified to discover that even this one had gone.

Those people seem to be running a sort of pets' abbatoir.

Another letter was sent to me by the writers, and very agreeable it is too. But there is slightly more than anyone might need to know about their dog:

> BECKY'S TOE. *Becky decided she was going to see me off to America in a big way. Four days before leaving, she hurt her right paw quite badly, while playing with Jimmy on the rough track. The next day it was hot and swollen so on Monday I took her to the vet. An X-ray revealed that she had broken one of the small bones of her toe into three pieces. Because of the awkward site, our vet bound the wound rather than set it in plaster. He recommended weekly visits to check the paw…*

This goes on for quite a lot longer, encompassing the use of first aid by the husband, the dog chewing off the dressing, and the second X-ray, until you find yourself thinking that it may not be terribly interesting in itself, but it is certainly an insight into their lives.

Often round-robinners can tell you more than you really need to know:

> OUR *saddest news was the passing of our dear Sami.* [Cat? Dog? Goldfish? Iguana? We are not told.] *She had become steadily frailer during the year and when a blood test proved that her kidneys were 'shot' and that there was some liver damage, we knew a*

decision was close. Finally she had a problem with the bowels, and
we knew we couldn't wait any longer...

Here is a similarly sad letter about a rabbit with, it appears,
strange telepathic powers:

WE HAVE *had a year of rabbits, after Louisa wanted ONE last*
year, plus a friend — we ended up with four babies. We bought tiny
dog harnesses and extending leads, so they could run up the paths
of the garden and the lawns. We lost the mother in the hottest day
of the summer. Having taken Sasha and her mate out for a run in
the afternoon, Louisa said that it was too hot, and we decided to
run them all in the cool of the evening. Sasha did not want to do
anything but sit and stare at the hedge. When we put her into her
hutch, she just flopped in. I said there was something wrong, but
Andy said it was just the heat. (Sasha was Andy's favourite pet.) The
next morning Louisa went to let them out at about 7.45 a.m., and
came in crying that Sasha was dead. I jumped out of bed and
looked at my watch. It had stopped at 10.30 the evening before. I
asked Andy at what time we had put them away last night, and he
said 10.30. It really upset me, as I felt she had been trying to tell
me she was ill, and I had let her down. The battery on my watch had
run down at that specific time.

The woman at Rabbit Rescue [fascinating to know that such
an organization exists. I doubt that it has many branches
in Australia.] *told me that lop-eared rabbits suffer from strokes,*

due to the way they are created. She said that to create them, their skulls are crushed and their ears pulled through. This makes them suffer strokes. It really upset me...

No, please! I really didn't need to know that.

Sometimes the letters are quite charming, as is the one that gives this book its title.

MOST *of you know that we are great opera buffs and love to have opera playing on the CD while we are at home. The children have just got a new hamster, and we have noticed that whenever we play Verdi or Mozart or Wagner, he sits still, doing nothing or just nibbling on his food. But whenever we play Puccini, he leaps onto his wheel and starts spinning joyfully.* One Fine Day, *or* Your Tiny Hand, *all get him going.* On With The Motley *or the* Liebestod *just leave him cold.*

A slight element of excusable exaggeration there, I suspect.

Many people find that the muse of poetry comes knocking at their door in the festive season. She should always be sent away, without so much as a mince-pie. She is not welcome. She leads to stuff like this, from the American West:

THIS *year brought us blessings which we will tell,*
Doug's recovery from surgery last December went well,
As to Belinda and Dad's head-on crash with the car,
We're thankful their injuries weren't worse by far...

April found us in England with sister-in-law Pru,
Where to visit her mother in Exeter we flew.
We walked on the footpaths and hiked on the moor,
And met the wonderful people of England, for sure...

At this point they run out of rhymes, or perhaps just children, and are reduced to a shortened verse:

Jacqui's doing her Masters at San Francisco State,
Darlene's research continues on yeast's DNA trait,
While Jan's work is a challenge, in Boston, as of late.

Our greatest blessings we saved for the last —
Our family increased by two in the six months past.
Warren Randolph's birth was the 30th of May,
To Dirk and Connie, at eight pounds did he weigh.

For many people, cramming the required number of syllables into each line, as well as finding rhymes, is just too difficult. Others manage to get the scansion more or less right, though the effect can be ruined by the banality of the material. T. S. Eliot could write about lunch in a hotel; the rest of us are less felicitous:

Now Jack is manager of the bar in Leeds's Stafford Hotel,
And Hattie has a part time job there, waitressing, as well.
She's nearly finished her degree; hotel management will be new,

So together they are hoping that their dream will soon come true...

Stephen and his partner, Miranda is her name,
Still spend their time on DIY, no room is now the same.
They've even done the garden, which used to be so bare,
But now it's full of flowers and trees with Miranda's tender care.
'Do come and see us, Mum and Dad, because we have no car.
We need to go to B&Q, it isn't very far.'

These people from Australia stretch the poetic form to its very limit:

THERE was a 'young' couple from 'Strayya
Who decided to go right awayya
To England and Wales
And Scotland and a-else,
To see family and those much, much grayya...

On returning to Oz,
They stopped off, because
Japan, specially Kyoto, said 'hiyya!'
The temples were 'Wow!!!'
The bullet train — 'POW!!!'
But a day — far too short — for a stayya.

At this point, inspiration deserts them and they return to prose:

They've just seen their builder,
With persuasion have willed a
Nice draughtsman to draw up some initial floor plans and
elevations as the first step to finalizing the details and submitting
the official plans to the council.

And back again:

Next summer — out here,
(Construction so near)
Our new home will be happening — just 'cos!

But that is no more bold and unconventional than these people who write in free verse, making an agreeable change.

IN summer we camped alone in a woodland yurt where peace came
                                                    dripping slow,

Long walks in autumn.
Rams tupped the ewes.
Spotty died.
Tick and Boo came to stay.
Francis and Sarah got married.
Even under heavy snow we see snowdrops and some new growth.
In the East we saw rhubarb already.
In the summer we eat cucumbers.

The last line has a fine elegiac ring.

Some people send verses designed to cheer up the recipient, though one fears it might have the opposite effect. This is also from Australia:

SMILING *is infectious,*
You catch it like the 'flu,
When someone smiled at me today,
I started smiling too.

I passed around the corner and someone saw my grin.
When he smiled I realized I'd passed it onto him.

I thought about that smile, then I realized its worth.
A single smile, just like mine, could travel round the earth.

So, if you feel a smile begin, don't leave it undetected.
Let's start an epidemic quick, and get the world infected!

Reading that can leave you with a rictus grimace, strangely similar to, yet very different from a smile.

One family sent their news in the form of a crossword, which can only be solved if you know the answers already. As the recipient says, 'We are supposed to know the family's life in all its ghastly detail and spend time trying to sort out the clues and answers.' And the clues are quite baffling: 'Thereby hangs a tail (in our house) (4)'. What is that – the name of a pet? 'Two pigs of this kind have recently joined our household (6)'; 'We love to play this game together (6)'; 'One route to our newly renovated attic (4,4)' What can that be? Roof lift? Rope pull? I suppose you could squeeze in 'loft ladder' if you wrote really small. 'Airport we have never flown from (5)'. Who can possibly guess? Luton? Paris? Quito? Why on earth should anyone want a Christmas newsletter that only tells you what the news is if you already know it?

Some people, possibly in response to the mockery evoked these days by round robins, have begun to send very short ones.

A BRIEF *summary of the year: Madeleine gave birth to Scarlett (1st July), Edward moved jobs (to Nottingham), Edward eventually became Dr Edward, we all moved house.*

Or this, from a reader:

WE HAVE *received what may possibly the shortest Christmas letter we have ever received. We have not heard from these people since last Christmas. It reads entirely 'Henry has broken his arm'. After some thought, we realized that Henry's wife was writing the cards this year for the first time.*

Some are just sad:

SORRY, *no newsletter this year, as we lost my sister Josie in September. Best wishes for the festive season.*

One especially poignant letter reads, in its entirety:

2004. Don't even ask.

Some are genuinely funny. I liked this spoof from California:

KYLE *took down our boxes of antique decorations late last night from the attic. The mice had eaten them all! But the good news is that a window in the attic had been open and the mice had all frozen to death. The mice are remarkably preserved and look so cute, we are going to use them as decorations this year. Aren't we creative?*

This is from a Welsh family, writing about their life and thoughts on current events:

THERE *are many eccentricities in British politics, but the oddest of the lot must be the Liberal Democrat who was sacked as a frontbench spokesman when she said that if she were a Palestinian, she might become a suicide bomber herself. Less widely reported was that a Palestinian suicide bomber had caused equal outrage by saying that if she were British, she might just become a Liberal Democrat MP. She was called in by the Hamas chief whip, and had her bomb withdrawn…*

Some are simply baffling:

TOM *informs the world that his current thesis topic is in the area of cyborg research (artificial bone replacements) and that he is still going by the pseudonym Ethel. He maintains a fairly active online*

presence, and can be contacted at EthelTheHut@btinternet.com
for those truly desperate to get in touch with him.

This is part of a long letter from a Welsh gay. It includes cheery descriptions of trips to Budapest, London, Helsinki, Estonia and Tenerife. He also goes off walking with a Welsh gay rambling association, which has managed to get special permission to traverse land owned by the Ministry of Defence.

OUR group was the first to sample some very beautiful scenery. We
still needed MoD permission and we were warned not to pick
anything up. I nearly asked 'do you mean unexploded grenades, or
16-year-old squaddies? Well, both can go off in yer hand!'

Thank you for that. I think we'll finish there.

The Sophistry of Sanctimony

'How is it,' asks one of my correspondents, 'that everything good that happens can be credited to God, but He is in no way to blame for the bad things?' It is something of a mystery, often apparent but rarely explained, in a sub-genre of the Christmas round robin – the letter of praise and thanksgiving. For some people the news of their lives over the previous twelve months merely serves as top dressing for the real business: the message of Jesus Christ.

One is loath to make fun of people's religion, but it is sometimes strange that suffering the most horrible illness will actually strengthen people's faith, while never once leaving them to question how they were allowed to become ill in the first place.

Some are unexceptional, making parts of their letters merely seem like the peroration in a rather dreary C of E sermon:

> So, another year gone, another year older. Probably not wiser, but a
> wide range of experiences to look back on with joy, sadness,
> frustration or simply fondness. Most importantly, however, we look
> forward to the annual but always fresh celebration of the birth of
> Christ. Undimmed by repeated carol services, or the frustrations of
> church politics, we can still join with the angels and experience

*afresh the message of goodwill and the promise of salvation,
brought especially at Christmas, but with us forever... our prayers
are with you.*

Some make their entire letter a hymn to the Lord. This one, from
a doctor's family in the south-east, is decorated with texts, apparently thrown in at random:

*... THE wedding dress is bought, and plans are already well
advanced, as you can imagine. Jesus said 'I am the light of the
world'... real advances have been made in developing national
guidelines and standards for patients in A&E departments. The
Executive Committee has also been a good experience. Life is full of
joy and challenge but we only have one life to give, just as Jesus
only had one life to give. He gave his life for us, so let us give our
life for Him...*

The wife, Janet, takes over the narration:

*I have managed to travel overseas fourteen times for one purpose or
another in the last twelve months. It has been an exhilarating
experience, which leaves me with the question: 'Lord, what do you
want me to do with my time?'*

She ruptures an Achilles tendon while playing squash in February,
so the answer to that question seems to be 'lie in bed in a plaster
cast'. One of their daughters is a midwife, and is going to Thailand

for the purpose of rescuing young prostitutes, 'getting them off the streets and giving them a future in Jesus (and a different job!).'

The family goes to the Bahamas for a holiday:

> *This was nearly a disaster, due to the hurricane, but God had mercy on us and managed to rearrange the whole thing in the last two days before departure.*

Does she seriously believe that God rearranged the path of the hurricane purely in order to avoid spoiling their holiday? Or is this Janet's ever so subtle jibe at the rest of the family? It is impossible to know. Or take this:

> *June saw me operated on for gall-bladder removal. The surgeon said it took a bottle of whisky that evening to help him get over it. Evidently, when he got 'in there' he found adhesions from former operations, and he had to fillet his way through to get a gall bladder. With prayer support as I had, he could not fail. I still sport a lovely long red scar across my tum...*

That letter, dated December 2004, also includes the surprising but apparently true fact that they have a granddaughter in Australia whose parents named her, some time before Boxing Day 2004, 'Tsunami'.

But it is quite clear that, for religious folk, even if God doesn't prevent them from becoming ill, He moves promptly into action when they are:

AROUND *the same time, some fleeting symptoms prompted Norman to visit the GP. It was lucky he did, because the symptoms lasted thirty-six hours. In May, he was diagnosed with kidney cancer. Unbelievably, we had only one sleepless night, punctuated by numerous nocturnal cups of tea. We then realized that in a wonderful way we are being looked after. People from all round the world prayed for Norman, and our faith convinced us that things would continue to go well.*

The hospital invited Norman to spend ten to fourteen days recovering from surgery, but they had had enough after three days and sent him home – minus his right kidney and its 'hanger-on'. Apparently this was a record. He didn't even miss one Sunday at our local church, and caused one poor old lady to fall off her seat when he reappeared much earlier than expected!

These people seem to have rediscovered Christian Science. After the usual round of house conversions and successful children, the wife writes:

I HAVE *been organizing Christian conferences on 'Creativity – Restoring the Soul'; 'The Prophetic' and 'Restoration Healing'. The numbers attending have increased each time and we are expecting a hundred in February for a Healing Conference. It has been wonderful and so rewarding to see people released from fears, bondages, trauma, etc.*

The highlight of my year was when another friend and myself

*prayed for a woman, Annie, who had Multiple Chemical Allergy
and had been confined to one room for five to six years. A ghastly
'modern' disease in which people are allergic to any type of
chemical smell, including soap, hairspray, cleaning fluids, etc.
Anyway, the Lord completely healed her!! Six months later she is
still extremely well and enjoying a normal life. Hallelujah!*

Or take this:

KATIE's *seasonal entertainment job has finished for now, so she is
selling shoes in faith, at Debenhams, and loving it!!! She buys just
as many as she sells.*

Which leaves you to wonder how you sell shoes in faith. 'Madam
might prefer this hard-wearing style; it has an immortal sole,'
perhaps. (An apology: I have just been told that 'faith' is a shoe-
store within Debenhams.) The letter goes on:

*Sadly, one of my girl pupils, Vienna, was killed in a car crash while
celebrating her ninth birthday in New Zealand, visiting Jake, her
big brother, who was on a gap year there. Sadly Jake was driving.
Tania, their mother, is still wearing a metal contraption on her
head. The children and I had a memorial service for Vienna, and my
headteacher actually praised me! As Tania and Jake approach their
first Christmas since Vienna's death, I would ask my Christian
friends to pray for them, please.*

Oh dear, one doesn't want to be cynical, but it does appear that faith can be a kind of WD-40, to be sprayed onto all of life's difficulties, great and small. True faith seems to involve attributing almost every good thing in your life to the Lord's beneficent help:

> SPEAKING *of co-incidences, or God's hand, Chery was on a plane going to Chicago for a business meeting, and guess who the flight attendant was? Tiffany Bayliss, her aunt!*

Religious people find religion everywhere they go.

> WHEN *I walked down our main shopping street on Victorian Night, I was very impressed by a group of youngsters about seventeen to nineteen years old playing music and singing the songs I have on my latest worship tape in the car... Tamsin, my shyest daughter, has just started a Christian Union course and her non-Christian friends go along.*

This letter, from north-west England, is a chapter of medical mayhem, relieved only by religious faith:

> IT HAS *been a very strange year for Harold and myself. In March he woke up one morning with chest pains and was taken to hospital, where I was told he was having a heart attack! All I could think was, I can't believe this is happening. I cried out to Father God, who saw my tears and heard my prayer for help. I felt His comfort and knew His peace. If you have time, read Psalm 25. Harold said he*

was at peace all the time, and kept repeating Psalm 25. I don't honestly know how people manage without faith in a Living God!

After four days of intensive care, Harold was allowed home, with the verdict possibly angina. A few weeks later his father, aged ninety-one, died and my mother fell and bruised her hip. She couldn't walk and had to use a wheelchair. We cancelled our holidays around the Greek islands... a few months later Harold was waiting to cross the road and a van ran right into the back of him, causing whiplash and a written-off van!

We must not expect life to be just. Christianity does not teach that it is; we live in a fallen world, and our prayer should not be for justice in life, but for God's help to turn every pain into a pearl. On a brighter note our grandchildren, Toby and Cameron, are very much involved in football... and enjoying all the beauty God has created.

It can be slightly alarming to discover whole families of devout people. Don't the children ever get tempted to cut loose and let rip? Only up to a point. These people from the north-east have each member of the family make a contribution, starting with the wife, who had heart problems:

IT took the following five weeks off work to accept that doing three jobs, plus being a Mum, wife, preacher and popular agony aunt for a year could constitute 'stress'.

His faith helps her husband through it all.

Walking, praying weekly, with a friend and psychotherapy have been anchors in the storm...

Their older boy starts by sounding like any other teenager:

The last year has been great for me! In January I became interested in Warhammer 40,000. This is a battle game set in the 41st millennium. I have been collecting an army of Chaos Space Marines. I then went on to discover P.O.D., a Christian metal band, and have had loads of fun listening to them. Harvest, a Christian youth camp, has been a great help spiritually, and a chance to get away from Mum and Dad... school has been tiring, but God, Mum, Dad and my brother have helped me pull through.

His younger brother reports an interest in skateboarding and rugby.

It was my first year at Harvest this year. Boy, it was great! Just a few days ago I was at a Christian rock concert called ixth hour *(ninth hour). This, combined with Harvest, have made me (a) wonderfully refreshed in God's spirit, and (b) extremely tired.*

For some people, God's involvement in their life is merely an extension of every other satisfactory circumstance, such as the promotion at work, the talents of their offspring, and the new water feature in the garden. These people have a wonderful holiday in Brazil.

IN RIO, we goggled at the views and the huge, famous statue of
Christ the Redeemer, nail prints and all, another moving
experience... on our last day we bravely went up in cable cars and
near the top we could hear singing – former members of Yale's
choral society were on tour. As the sun went down, the clouds parted
and the Christ appeared, and with the singing in the background,
that was a very special moment. The Lord had been so good to us
throughout the trip.

Would that be the same Lord that arranged for the earlier couple
to cancel their Greek holiday because of family illness?

One reader writes in exasperation from the Home Counties:

MY all-time favourite letter came from an old university friend
who is now a born-again Christian. Annually we get to hear of
God's purpose in their lives, though He wasn't responsible for their
eldest son being mugged. That's the trouble with Christianity – it is
never God's fault. Anyway, the classic sentence (I no longer have the
original) refers to some happy-clappy musical they put on at their
church:

'I never thought I would dance in church, but God had other
ideas!'

Aaargh!

Some of the scarier letters come from the United States. This, for
example, is from an American air force family, and most of it con-

sists of reunions, trips to visit old military friends, holidays and funerals. Then suddenly:

> WITH *the Episcopal church in the USA in freefall towards the fellow with red horns, the Church of Christ the King is a refreshing island in a sea of effluent. God willing, it will stay that way. We assume with the new election of a heretic to the San Diego Bishop's office, the final battle may be sooner rather than later.*

That sounds a little threatening.

Some people are into a form of vague, miasmic mysticism. This, not surprisingly perhaps, is from California:

> IN *2005, we enter the twenty-second year of our Mystery School. How about that? Twenty-two years of continuous adventures and journeys of mind, body and spirit into the mystery of who and what we are, and what we yet may be. Twenty-two years of a bonded, cherishing community and training in what makes life worthwhile. Twenty-two years of what many have called the best school in the world.*
>
> *Many have lost their sense of who, why and what we are in the face of so many challenges for which most of us have been unprepared. Our purpose and destiny are shrouded in mystery, and it will take the hardy traveler into the mind and soul's deepest continents to rediscover the path that leads to the greening of this world and time. This is why the Mystery School is dedicated to the*

new journey of our lives, during which we will find the maps
and enter together into the places where our deepest purposes
touch the emergent new story that is struggling to enter into
time...

What's that? Sorry, I was miles away...

This is from a woman in New York City who doesn't waste much time in getting down to the spiritual sales pitch.

... I ALSO continue to sing in the Voices of Unity and have begun a
two-year interfaith seminary program. What is interfaith, you may
ask? It is the study of all religions in order to understand our
commonalities rather than our differences. At this time, it is more
necessary than ever. If you believe this is something worthwhile and
wish to contribute to the study and to my work in it, you can make
an end of the tax year write-off to One Spirit Interfaith, and send
it to me.

At least she doesn't include a tear-off slip at the bottom.

The final letter in this section is extraordinary. It is approximately 6,200 words long and comes from a British family now farming in New Zealand. Indeed, it is so long that it could easily serve as an instruction manual for anyone setting up a farm in New Zealand, blended seamlessly with a devotional volume about God's goodness.

For He is everywhere.

WE are most grateful to our family for the wonderful day they
organized, and we are keenly looking forward to our next wedding
anniversary now! However, the future belongs to our Heavenly
Father...

   During the past two months we have been busy catching up with
various tasks, in particular semi-permanent fences of fibre-glass
rods and two electrified high-tensile steel wires, on both sides of the
drains that are like small canals, as in the past someone had made
them too wide... also it is best to stop the stock drinking from
them, as they tend to damage the sides and make them even wider.
Gideon has also made some fresh crossings of the drains that make
stock moving much easier at flood time. We also plan to make three
cattle races during the next few weeks using poly rods and wire. The
electric fence improvements should cut our routine electric fence
moving by about 60 per cent or more, next we plan to subdivide
more of the paddocks with poly rods...

   Our sheep mainly live on the hills, we also enjoy mustering
them, watching them follow the leaders, we do not use dogs, just
quietly follow them, they seem to be becoming much more friendly.
We hope they will eventually learn to come when called, by
recognizing our voices, as they did in Biblical times...

And so the life of the farm goes on, day after day after day, all
described in the minutest detail. But that doesn't mean they have
no time for fun and socializing.

Recently we went to an excellent presentation about sharing the
good news of the Saviour in Arab countries by folk who had lived
and worked in North Africa and the Middle East for many years.
While fundamental Islam is lethal, it was thought that overall only
2 per cent of the total Arab population actually had a heart belief
in Islam. The other 98 per cent believed in something else, or at
least were only nominally Muslim.

And so the life of the farm goes on, and on. Now and again they
are able to look at the wider picture:

Most New Zealanders are appalled at the moral landslide affecting
the country, though trends are comparable to most of the rest of the
Western world. New Zealand, like the rest, has suffered from
decades of humanistic socialism, liberal education and the so-called
women's lib. The promotion of evolution as a fact rather than as a
theory — in the media as well as places of learning, has done much
to undermine Godly values and attitudes. The West is now reaping
its fruit.

They finish with a few thoughts on the role of the European Union
and how, in league with the British government, it is destroying
British farming – which might well be true. Indeed, a sign comes
from an unlikely source:

Walking on the hills, we surprised a lone sheep who had lost sight
of her flock. So startled did she look that I asked her, 'what's the

matter, then?' She eyed me for a moment or two, then uttered a very distinct 'blair' before bolting off. She left me wondering if she had deep political insight.

Then, after nine closely typed A4 pages, they finish with a personal note to their addressees:

We hope you have a lovely holiday together. Gideon has prepared some photos to go with this.

Really? Has he? Do tell him to take his time, there's absolutely no rush...

The Vice of Vituperation

I PERSONALLY don't hate round robin letters, even the ones we receive at home – though not many of them arrive these days. They can be annoying, though more often unintentionally hilarious. After all, you don't have to read every one of those computer specifications, the list of the children's GCSEs, or the minute-by-minute account of the holiday in Peru. And there is a certain *schadenfreude* to be extracted from the things that have gone terribly wrong. Some of these are merely hinted at: 'Emily brings joy and laughter to our lives', if unaccompanied by a list of academic qualifications and musical accomplishments, can indicate learning difficulties.

But other recipients of the letters are less tolerant. For me, among the delights of being sent so many hundreds of letters every year are the covering notes, some of them almost literally smothered in rage and bile. For example, one dated from Christmas 2004 has five chunks torn out of it. The reader has written over the top: 'our dog felt the same way about this letter, and tried to eat it'. Small wonder, since it includes some particularly infuriating paragraphs, such as this about the senders' twenty-one-year-old son:

He has been taken on by a US conglomerate based in Slough. He is being paid a fantastic salary and has his own desk, telephone, parking space et al. His title is marketing assistant, and involves travelling all over the UK to give presentations to oil and electricity generating bigwigs. When his line manager is abroad, he is allowed to drive the company car (Jaguar or Saab).

Here's another typical example of recipient rage:

I enclose a round robin letter which would not fail to bore you stupid. I left their home town over ten years ago and hardly knew the children mentioned, so I found the whole letter smug, boring, and of no interest whatsoever. Sorry if I sound unkind.

No, please don't apologize!

At least the Parkers can be relied on for consistency – they are all still gifted, multi-talented, and smug!

The Parkers' letter caused extra fury, since near the end it reveals that the sender's husband is about to sack almost all the workforce in his company. A typically jaunty paragraph reads:

Andy and his brother have concluded that the business is unsustainable, and are now in the process of all but closing it, reducing to about 10 per cent. It's a blow they cannot help but take on a personal level. Their dad founded the company in 1947, average length of service is twenty years, some employees have never

worked anywhere else, and many are each other's fathers, brothers,
nephews and in-laws. Let's hope this difficult decision will prove a
move for the better for everyone.

As the recipient writes in her covering letter:

THE FACT *that he is sacking 90 per cent of his workforce rates just*
this one short paragraph. I just hope none of the employees are on
her mailing list.

If they were, they would receive along with their P45s jolly news
of the family's skiing trips to the Alps and their luxurious holiday
in Sorrento.

Other letters create feelings of nausea which are just as strong
for different reasons.

PLEASE *find enclosed a truly horrific round robin, which you can*
use in your new book Christmas With The Fokkers. I shared a flat
with Jenny in the early 70s, and I can only think that she has either
had a frontal lobotomy or has embraced Stepford principles
wholeheartedly.

THIS *letter was sent by a person with whom I had a brief fling*
thirty years ago. It ended entirely without acrimony, but it did end
with total finality, and we have had no communication with each
other since — apart, that is, from the Christmas newsletter, which
started turning up about eight years ago. The thing is that there are

*fourteen or fifteen people mentioned in the letter – at least I
assume they are all people. I suppose 'Edith' could be a faithful old
sheepdog – and I have not the remotest idea who any of them are.*

I AM *enclosing this year's offering from Vanessa, which I always
find cloying and yucky. Unfortunately, the letter does not show how
very, very clever Vanessa must be, as she's been writing to us every
year since she was a foetus.*

Some people are more inclined to resent the time and effort
implied by being sent these letters. Why, they ask, should I use
energy I could be devoting to watching *Celebrity Love Island* or
watching paint dry?

THESE *people's letters always induce a great depression in me. I
particularly liked the part about the garden, with the two
indistinguishable 'before' and 'after' pictures.*

Indeed the pictures are almost identical, with one barely noticeable difference:

BEFORE *the summer we did a bit of work in the garden. At the end
of the lawn at the back we have a number of Leylandii. Nothing
much grows under them, so we decided to replace the weeds with
decorative stones and plants in pots. We also got a composter. It is to
the left of the view above. It took only a few weeks to fill it up, and
we have not yet taken any compost out of it. The amount of grass*

cuttings produced would fill a dozen composters, so we still have to make trips to the refuse tip with the excess.

Or here is the account of their summer holiday. It is clear that the family as a whole is close to losing the will to live; what maddens the readers is the sense that they wish to transfer their malaise to everyone else:

This summer we spent twelve nights camping in France. This was at the back end of August, when it rained just about every day. The intention was to have an easy, beach-based holiday as the camp site was only a short walk from the beach. We did manage a couple of days in the sun. We sailed from Portsmouth to Cherbourg and drove down to Dinard, which is near St Malo. As we could not spend much time on the beach we drove to various towns in the area. We went to Fougères, Saint Suliac, Dinan and Mt. St. Michel. The girls could practise their French buying bread and croissants every morning on the site. Isobel has since started doing French at school and is getting on well...

Please, no more! It is unsurprising that some recipients seem driven to the edge of their reason by these letters. It's hard to know what is more aggravating – boastfulness or boringness. Take this letter from Canada which brought much grief to the English people who received it:

How *are things with us? Well, as Canadians, we tend to be upbeat*

about everything! So the answer is 'Good!' A while ago, I asked a
friend who is more dour than most, 'How's it going?' He replied,
'good and bad'. That is probably about as honest and complete an
answer as anyone can give. And we're all likely the same. But for
those of you who are interested, here is a rundown of what we have
done in the last year. There has been so much to be thankful for, and
yet some things that we wish could have been better.

By this time, the average recipient is in a deep and peaceful trance.
But other letters create the opposite effect, sending fiery currents
of rage coursing through the readers' veins.

I CAN hardly begin to tell you about my feelings for these
appalling people. Please put them in your next book and name
them! Why should they get away with it? I only know them because
I was at school with her. She was head girl, and had a huge bosom. I
haven't seen her in twenty years, thank God, but I bet the bust is of
double-decker proportions now.

Rich, smug and revolting, 42-foot yachts, perfect house, bloody
great mediaeval barns — can it get any worse? I want to kill them.
Mind you, I think that every time their hideous newsletter arrives,
and then next year's offering comes along, and it is always worse. I
suppose we'll have the details of the sodding wedding next time
round... Oh God, I can't go on. Even writing about them makes
me ill.

The powerful desire to mete out death to letter-writers is a frequent theme:

> IT's *the all-round smugness that gets me. They are both senior*
> *lecturers and nice people — till now! This made me want to go*
> *round and throttle them.*

Some people find news from the former colonies particularly grating:

> THIS *classic example is hot off my aunt's printer in Adelaide. It is,*
> *yet again, more badly constructed and punctuated drivel. As if*
> *having to read such sublime comments as 'it was very biblical in*
> *places like Damascus and Mount Sinai' wasn't enough, she goes on*
> *to write about our lives in the UK!*

Which she does, complacently describing how her mother-in-law has been helped by the installation of a new stairlift — and sending this information to the very people who arranged for it to be installed, without giving them credit for their work.

But telling people news about themselves can be a hazard in letters sent to dozens, perhaps hundreds. One reader writes from a rectory in Lancashire:

> I WAS *reminded of a newsletter I received some years ago while*
> *working abroad. It was from a well-meaning but busybody family I*
> *knew slightly, and ran to several sides of A4. I was faintly surprised*

even to receive the letter, and very surprised to read an entire
paragraph in it about me, along the lines of 'our minister's wife
is...' with full details of what I was doing, why and where, written
by people I barely knew for people I had never met. That felt weird.

Almost as weird as the chap in Somerset must have felt when he got a lengthy newsletter, with the death of his own wife tucked away in half a paragraph, crammed in amid the news of exotic holidays and the addition of a new sun lounge:

... ALSO the death of our dear friend Carol, who put up a brave
struggle against lymphoma. Our thoughts are with Nigel and his
sons this Christmas...

... they wrote to Nigel.

A new menace is the website Friends Reunited. It was through them that a couple in Essex began to receive round robins from another couple who had been fellow pupils in the wife's primary school class fifty-five years ago. She had not met them during the course of the following five and a half decades.

THIS letter is typical, exhorting us to think more about other
people than ourselves, to be grateful for our many blessings, and
usually ending with a little homily leaving us in no doubt about
what selfish people we are. I can just about stomach the fact that
they enjoy a direct line to the Lord, but the overall sanctimonious
tone makes me feel quite unwell.

And you can see her point:

> IN JUNE *we had our second Scarecrow Festival, with our tiny hamlet producing another sixty different scarecrows. It was highly successful and the Good Lord looked very kindly on us with a weekend of sunshine, and it was dry underfoot from the previous week. Austin has kept records of our weather down here for the last ten years, and they make interesting reading. We have had more rain this year. Unfortunately we do not have the means of measuring the sunshine… this year we have decided to donate to charity instead of giving gifts. It seems that all of us who have so much should share it with those who have nothing.*

Thank you for that thought, which of course had never occurred to any of us.

As the chapter on religion shows, many people imagine that the Almighty personally arranges the weather for their convenience and delight.

> BACK *in July Dad was eighty, so we had a celebration meal. Church friends joined him and Mum, as well as other close friends. It was a good day, and the Lord blessed us with lovely weather and we were able to enjoy the beautiful grounds, with the wildlife and the lake. We were left very well fed, and not wanting to eat the following day.*

An effect not uncommon among the readers of such letters. As the recipient of that one wrote:

THE LAST *time I saw this person was eight years ago, and she*
subsequently accused me — without explaining to me what I was
supposed to have done — of having spoiled her parents' fiftieth
anniversary party. Do you suppose that perhaps the continued
despatch of these letters might be seen as a form of prolonged
punishment?

It is curious how a complete lack of response rarely makes a difference to the senders of round robins.

THIS *arrives every year addressed to my parents, who are both*
dead. It is from the daughter of a very distant (and also dead)
friend of my mother's, and she hated receiving the letter every year.
The senders do not provide their address, so I cannot return it
unopened and so stop this annual torment!

Occasionally the letters are not so terrible — at least not as bad as
some others. That does not stop their unlucky readers from
foaming at the mouth, biting the arms of sofas, barking at the dog,
and so forth.

I THINK *you might agree that the whole tone of this letter is self-*
serving, and designed to create an impression of general all-round-
aren't-we-super-people-ness. There are two paragraphs that really
do it for me, though. One is the totally pointless reference to staying
in 'Landmark Trust property number 20', and the other has to be
the unbelievable '. . . we spotted some more stars at Jani's [who the

hell is Jani?] opening night… but more importantly saw her to be
a star'. The final joy of that phrase is the comment in brackets:
'(Dave is now engaged to Selma)', like a conspiratorial aside to the
knowing. And I don't know any of them!

So, apart from discovering that they had chicken pox, stayed in a
lot of posh properties, and hob-nobbed with famous people such as
Rick Stein, I have learned that the wife is doing terribly well with
her choreography, does selfless work for the community and
combines raising 'two gorgeous chaps' with full-time work at The
Elms. What a woman. How nice of her to let me know…

Oh dear, I feel that the sender should be more careful next year, and get someone else to pre-read the letter, otherwise cardiac arrest might result.

Some people also relish the bad news.

I DON'T know how many Christmas letters you get with pictures of
legs with bolts through them, but here is one. The mother's delight
at the violence of injury to her daughter can be attributed to her
nursing training…

And the details are in the letter:

MARTHA was off to Pony Club for a week, and this is where the
drama started! On the second day she was involved in a very bad
accident when the horse fell back on her and broke her leg (the
right femur was snapped clean in two.) She was blue-lighted to

hospital by ambulance, and underwent minor surgery to stick a bolt
through the bottom of her shin so she could go on traction (see
right)...

And there it is, for the delectation of all her parents' acquaintance:
a young girl's leg with a Frankenstein's monster-style bolt through
it.

However, it's intriguing how newsletter writers are often slow
to show concern about other people's mishaps.

I ENCLOSE *a round robin letter from Somerset... this former*
friend has never once responded to my hand-written card telling
her that my husband had had a heart attack. I have merely had this
rubbish in reply. She is now struck off our Christmas card list, as
these letters make me so angry.

The rage sometimes just bubbles over:

THIS *letter, by my brother-in-law, is simply designed to make the*
rest of us know how tawdry and uninteresting our lives are
compared to the Campbells.

The accompanying missive, from Scotland, certainly starts in chal-
lenging fashion:

2004 *has been memorable in the Campbell nest for Poughkeepsie's*
mastery of disembowelling mice in total darkness. [Poughkeepsie
is a cat, named after the town in New York state]...

Nightly, at almost exactly 2 a.m., for the past six months, Angus
and Morag have been woken by the gently rhythmic cracking of
bones just inches from their unseeing eyes. At dawn, the first rays of
sun glint across the neatly dissected silhouette of the rejected
stomach on the pillow...

Thankfully, the rest of the four-page letter reverts to the usual
parade of academic and sporting success, interrupted only by
costly and exotic holidays.

A reader from north London sends in two newsletters:

CLIVE *and Debs lived two doors away from me for four years. Their*
house was originally owned by her grandmother, who lived there for
many years and whom my mother and I knew on a polite,
neighbourly 'hello' basis. I had absolutely nothing in common with
them and found another polite 'hello' often best avoided, as any
ensuing conversation would always entail lengthy, self-centred
monologues from them.

Phyllis was Debs's mother, who died two years ago, and Roy, her
father, still lives in their house in the next road. I do not know him,
except by sight. He would not know me — thankfully! — and neither
would the dog, if you can call that a dog.

The picture implies that it is indeed a rather small and yappy-
looking canine. However, nothing prevents Roy from sending his
newsletter to a woman whom he would not even recognize if he

met her in the street. Like many older people, he does seem to lead a life of necessarily limited excitment:

> RECENTLY, *my faithful TV in its nice wooden cabinet (remember when all televisions were housed in wood? This one was over twenty years old) decided it had had enough and died on me. I thought that as I did not watch TV that often I would wait until the sales before replacing it, but strangely I missed them. So I splashed out on a nice new, up to date piece of equipment. I must say that TV sets have improved over the last twenty-plus years. I might enjoy watching TV and the occasional video, but not too much.*

But enjoying his new TV, though not too much, isn't all he does.

> *Musically, I continue with my accordion, including lessons. I also continue with visits to Glyndebourne…*

Without, one hopes, the accordion, which would not be welcomed during an adventurous new production of *The Magic Flute*.

Back to Clive and Debs who, it turns out, were great fans of Concorde:

> CONCORDE *has not disappeared from our lives, even though she is no longer flying. We have already visited the Manchester exhibit — Daisy finally got to see the inside of Concorde! There were many auctions held after her retirement* [Concorde's not Daisy's] *to sell off all the spares and memorabilia. We now have some bizarre*

items around the house and garden, including an exhaust gas temperature thermo-couple, three cockpit dials, an explosion detector, engine and reheat components, landing gear wheel rims — the list goes on. Some stuff we have purchased for resale, such as Concorde Sennheiser headphones, pens, cutlery, glasses and Wedgwood stuff.

However, the pinnacle of our collection has to be the TOILET CUBICLE!!! Which won us a piece in The Scotsman *newspaper, as well as a big article in the* Daily Express *— for some reason, the press find the idea of a Concorde toilet sitting in our lounge strangely and hilariously worthy of coverage…*

Hard to understand.

Another letter is the usual gallimaufry of examination successes, and superb holidays — in Peru (why do so many round robin writers wind up in Machu Picchu? Is it a sort of secret convention centre where they can share notes about how to infuriate their readers?) — plus trips to Portugal, Italy and Wales. Only one bad thing happens to any of them:

JANET *had a year of toothache, that ended with an hour and a half in the dentist's chair, and three nerves removed!*

As the recipient remarks:

OUR *feelings of indifference towards these people, who are our neighbours, have now been transformed into loathing, and a profound sorrow that the toothache has been cured.*

Some readers, by contrast, are consumed more by sorrow than by anger:

THIS *is from some very old friends, but I cannot help but feel slightly embarrassed for them, rather like overhearing a very elderly relative break wind at Christmas dinner.*

The letter referred to does include some rather sweet, even plangent lines:

FEWER *guests have visited this year, for no apparent reason.*

This next letter accompanied a round robin from landowners, who devoted it mainly to – no doubt well-justified – complaints about the DEFRA bureaucracy.

THE REFORM *of the Common Agricultural Policy and the finalization of the Scottish Outdoor Access Code reared their ugly heads and required much study...*

The recipients write:

THIS *letter was sent to us by a couple who we met twenty-five years ago and have not seen since. We receive the same ghastly letter every Christmas, relating their tales of woe and cattle or land purchases, interspersed with stories of their many holidays. They live in a castle in Scotland – see photo by their talented daughter.*

It all got too much for one of my own daughters three years ago,
so she returned their letter to them with the words, 'I believe you
have mistaken me for someone who gives a fuck.' She sent it
unsigned. In the past two years, my daughters have annotated the
letters and returned the first from Belfast, and the other from
Madrid.

Which is one way of getting your revenge.

Others include writing furious annotations in the margins of the
letters. For example, this letter tackles the writer's daughter and
son-in-law:

TERRY *is very clever, he has two degrees, also he just passed his*
Masters and his graduation is in two weeks. Elinor is different,
down to earth, basically not academic, doesn't care about that, but
has more sense than Terry. If you want anything organized, ask
Elinor. If you want a nail knocking in, ask Elinor. In fact, if you
want anything, ask Elinor, Terry is hopeless. It works, though, we
take him as he is, we've known him long enough now.

As the recipient writes, 'what is her poor son-in-law supposed to
make of this?'

Another form of revenge is to send spoof letters in return. The
theory is that these will subtly expose to the original senders how
ridiculous the concept can be.

EMILY *is back working in Manchester. She has a new pimp, which*